'There is only one part of the body the club is in contact with, and that is the hands'. Max Faulkner at moment of impact

Play Championship Golf
All Your Life

MAX FAULKNER
in collaboration with
TOM SCOTT

Illustrated with drawings by
PAUL TREVILLION

PELHAM BOOKS

First published in Great Britain by
PELHAM BOOKS LTD
52 Bedford Square
*London, W.C.*1
SEPTEMBER 1972
SECOND IMPRESSION MARCH 1973

© 1972 *by Max Faulkner*

ISBN 0 7207 0256 9

Printed in Great Britain by
Hollen Street Press Ltd at Slough
and bound by James Burn at Esher, Surrey

Contents

Illustrations

'There is only one part of the body the club is in contact with, and that is the hands.' Max Faulkner at moment of impact.

Foreword

by Tom Scott

For a quarter of a century or so, Max Faulkner has not only been one of the leading golf professionals in Britain, but has also been one of the most colourful and most popular. My first close association with him was on that memorable day at Royal Portrush in Northern Ireland, in 1951, when he won the Open Championship. Max finished with the total of 285 – which, when he walked off the last green, looked good enough to win. There was just one man who could beat him, Antonio Cerda from Argentina. Cerda was still out on the course, and the news that he was going well was too much for the usually laughing, joking Faulkner.

'I can't bear it,' he said to me. 'I just want to go somewhere away from everybody.'

'Right,' I replied, 'you come with me.' I managed to get him into the Steward's pantry in the Clubhouse. Not only that, but I also got him a pot of tea and then relayed to him the news of Cerda's progress. After what seemed hours I was able to go back to Max and tell him that Cerda had failed, and that he was the Open Champion.

I have many other memories of Max, but I will retell only one to prove to you – if any proof is needed – what a great sportsman he is. It was at the Ryder Cup match at Lindrick, in 1957. Great Britain had a bit of a hammering the first day and were 3–1 down in the foursomes. Max was playing with Harry Weetman. They lost their match and the captain, Dai Rees, dropped them from the side chosen for the singles on the following day, incidentally drawing from Harry a few well-chosen remarks.

There was no doubt that Max was disappointed, but every moment on that last day he ran round the course cajoling this one, bullying that one, encouraging the next one. It was partly due to him that his colleagues rose to the occasion, and scored one of the greatest and most dramatic victories in the whole history of the Ryder Cup.

As a player, he has had many wins to his credit, from the day that he won the Berkshire Championship as a young man of twenty-one, to his winning of the Seniors' Championship in 1970. In the world of golf he has long been acknowledged as a great player. He is also renowned as a great entertainer, and he is in much demand at Charity golf matches – not only for his skill as a golfer, but also as the man who persuades the crowd to fork out money for birdies and so on. Then, at the end of the round, he conducts the auction, and over the years he must have been responsible for various charities being richer to the extent of many thousands of pounds. His theory is, that if you get people laughing, they will give away money.

Then there is his manner of dress. If there was an annual award for the brightest dressed professional golfer on the fairways of the world, Max Faulkner must have been the winner many times. He always favours plus-fours, or I suppose you would call them plus-twos, and he seems to have a wide selection from which to choose, because it is nothing for him to appear in a red sweater and yellow knickerbockers in the morning and then, in the afternoon, to appear in a yellow sweater and mauve knickerbockers. And his stockings are of some similar dazzling colour.

How golf spectators would be disappointed, even hurt if they saw him appear in some sombre outfit. It would just not be Max. And he knows it.

In his younger days he was known as a great experimenter in various departments of golf, particularly in his putting, in which he has used many different implements. Some of his experiments succeeded, some failed. But always behind his thoughts there was something original. He did not just try out an experiment for the mere sake of trying it out. He tried it out after careful thought, and as a result be built up an unequalled knowledge of putting, in particular, and the game of golf in general.

In recent years he has given a great deal of study to golf, and decided that it was becoming much too complicated. He himself has always played golf in a simple manner and now, when in middle age, he hits the ball with great authority. In fact, it is true to say that there is no more stylish golfer on a golf course than Max Faulkner, and not so many more effective ones. Now, with his chicken farming and his fishing, he perhaps has not quite the keen appetite for competitive play that he once had. But his fine style is still with him, and the method he employs and the method he teaches is perfect for those who want to play golf successfully.

There is not the slightest doubt that golf has become most complicated, so complicated, in fact, that many of those taking up the game – and even those who have played it for some time – become utterly confused, sometimes even reaching the stage that those of weaker moral fibre give up the game altogether and those who have the will to carry on can only do so by starting all over again from the very beginning. The trouble with starting all over again is that they have to find a teacher who will teach them a simpler method than the one they used hitherto, otherwise they might well be in trouble again.

The great Ernest Jones, who was a Kent man but became one of the great golf coaches in the United States, always used to use a piece of nylon cord with a knife at one end, which he pulled out of his pocket to demonstrate just how simple golf was. He swung the cord backwards and forwards, and the knife performed a perfect arc.

'That,' Jones has told me many times, 'is just what golf is all about. It is as simple as that. What I am doing is making that knife go up and down in that arc. It is the same with golf. You have to make the clubhead do the work. It will not do it by itself. That is where so many golf teachers go wrong. They try to confuse their pupils by telling them this and that, when it is all perfectly straightforward'.

Max Faulkner has the same philosophy as Jones, although I doubt if he ever met him, and certainly he would never have seen him play. Jones' career as a golfer ended when he lost a leg in World War I. It was then he went to America and devoted himself to teaching.

One of the most controversial statements in this book is Max Faulkner's insistence that the club be taken back close to the ground allowing the clubhead to perform a wide arc. Nowadays a good number of the leading professionals do not do that. They raise the clubhead much more quickly, and, by their great strength, are able to bring the clubhead down in an effective way. But these men have, after some years, worked out their own method which suits them, and it does not mean to say that it will suit golfers of lesser skill, and those who, because they work in some sedentary occupation, have very much weaker hands than the pros who are playing in golf tournaments for money from one month's end to another.

This upright swinging of a golf club can cause trouble for many golfers who have not the technique or strength, and when something goes wrong – which it does from time to time

– such golfers are unable to cope with the problems which have presented themselves. If they kept to a simple basic method, they would, at least, have more chance of getting back on the right lines.

Max Faulkner is also critical of some professionals who teach the game for a living. In Britain there are many good golf professionals, but it is also a fact that there are many who are either moderate teachers or have little interest in standing for hours coaching club golfers. A few, I fear, have little qualification for teaching at all. After all, almost anyone can become a club professional, providing that he can get a club to employ him. And since, in some instances, the retainers paid by clubs are very small, the best man is not always appointed.

For a long time in Britain it has been advocated that there should be one basic form of golf instruction. In theory that would be excellent, but the question is, who is to thrash out the blue-print when professionals themselves cannot agree on a basic method?

Throughout the country there is a great divergence of opinion about teaching golf, and, golf being an individual game, that state of affairs is likely to continue, leaving the many golf professionals to teach pupils according to their own views.

I do not think for one moment that Max Faulkner believes that there is one way, and one way only, to hit a golf ball. At golf clubs one sees many players who can hit a golf ball a long distance with a most terrible style. But the question is, can he do it every time? With a bad and complicated style there is one thing which must be achieved, if the ball is to be hit straight and far, and that is bringing the clubhead into the ball square on and at maximum speed. A strong man can do it more often than not, but a weaker and less talented man can only do so occasionally.

In golf it is not good just playing good shots once in a while. That is why there are so many bad golfers, not only

13

in this country but all over the world. Max Faulkner's theory
is that the golf ball must be struck from the back, a theory
that makes commonsense to me, and to strike the ball from
the back instead of chopping down on it requires a wide arc.
And a wide arc can be achieved only in the manner which is
described in this book.

There may be some golfers who are very short, or very
stout, who will say that a wide arc is impossible for them. It
may be difficult, but it is not impossible, and such players will
certainly not get any better results by using their golf club
like a hatchet. In fact, playing like that is, for them, to court
disaster.

'Golf is a one-piece game' or 'Golf is the same from tee to
green' might well have been chosen as a title for this book,
because in Faulkner's opinion it is both of these things – an
opinion which will surprise many people who think that it
is a different game each time you use a different club. As
is clearly stated, golf is the same game throughout, except in
a very few instances. That viewpoint in itself helps to make
the whole thing simple.

But the simple way is not always the obvious way to
golfers who, for years, have been fed with theories, some of
them quite preposterous. In everyday life often quite easy
tasks are made more difficult just because the person doing
them thinks that there are some hidden complications. In
golf many people think exactly the same way.

Have you ever played a shot which sailed away right down
the fairway? And then, have you not been amazed because it
all went so smoothly and without effort? Of course you have.
What is not appreciated after such shots is that you have
done everything exactly right without thinking about a dozen
different things as you have taken the club back. This thinking about the various points in the golf swing causes more
bad shots than anything else, because the golf stroke, happen-
ing as it does in an instant, is over before the message your
brain has sent to the hands and the other parts of the body

has been properly sorted out. That being so, you try to think of more things in less time, and the result of it all is that your swing – if you can call it such – is quickened too.

But now I want to let Max speak for himself. I have read many, many golf books in my time, but I have rarely read one which is so revolutionary yet at the same time contains so much commonsense. I had some hand in the preparation and arranging of this book, but the text is Max Faulkner's own.

Those who know him and have heard him talk will be in no doubt about that because every line, every expression is easily recognisable as 'all his own work'.

He has been talked about wherever golfers meet for years, and I feel that this book is likely to have him talked about a great deal more. But before that has happened he is quite liable to have added to his already not inconsiderable total of money winnings on the golf course. 'Old soldiers', they say, 'never die, they only fade away.'

Although he makes wishes about that from time to time, there is no sign yet of Max fading away yet, and I feel that we shall see his sometimes outrageously dressed figure at tournaments and at exhibition matches for a long time to come. British sports lovers like their old favourites who gradually become a legend. Max Faulkner is already an almost legendary figure – one who has done much for the game of golf in Britain, and one who has given infinite pleasure to tens of thousands of people. His successor has not yet appeared on the horizon, and perhaps never will. That in itself, would not be surprising, because golfing extroverts of great skill do not grow on every tree.

The fact that he has played first-class golf for so long tells its own story. Some who have played in Ryder Cup teams with him, and in Ryder Cup teams since he last appeared, have faded from the scene – one or two of them because their technique were just not good enough. His own philosophy is that good golf cannot be played unless a golfer has a good technique, and a good technique, in his eyes, is a simple technique. In view of this long and distinguished career, who is to argue with him?

We hear much of the modern styles of the great Americans. But that must be put into its proper perspective. People point at the American stars and say: 'They are great because they play the right way.' But that is only half the story. Considering the difference in numbers between the United States and Britain, there are just as many moderate American club golfers as there are British. Without going into the reasons why the United States is the number one golfing nation, it cannot be said positively that the methods of the top men are any better than that of our top men. Let us leave it at that, for there is another point that is worth dwelling on: not many of their stars of yesteryear who are the same age as Max Faulkner play as well as he does, which is proof, if proof is needed, that his method is a good one.

And one other thing. Although Max Faulkner was born into golf – his father was a well-known professional – the method that he advocates is so simple that it must be suitable for ordinary club players and, perhaps most of all, for beginners.

Tom Scott.

Introduction

This book is going to surprise many golfers. It is going to upset dozens of professionals. But it just had to be written. You see, the game has got so complicated that the biggest percentage of ordinary club players have not the faintest idea of what they are trying to do, and why they are trying to do it.

They read articles in golf magazines, they read golf books, they go first to one professional and then to another, and in the end their heads are so full of what they have read and what they have been told that they are lost – and all mixed up. And no wonder, for now everybody seems to be trying to make golf the most complicated game on earth.

Much of the blame for this lies at the doorsteps of professionals teaching the game. They seem to think that when a pupil comes to them they have to give them value for money by using a lot of expressions that sound grand and mean nothing. Others get very technical and trot out such things as 'cocking the wrists', 'pronating', 'lateral movement' and the rest. No wonder the pupil – who, perhaps, cannot even get the ball off the ground – is mystified.

The trouble is that there are too many professionals teaching golf today who have no idea of what the game is all about. They pick up some 'gimmicks' and think they know everything. It makes me sad when someone comes and tells me what some professional has been teaching them. I have had golfers who have been going to a professional for weeks, perhaps months, in order to have a slice cured. I can cure a slice in one lesson. I can guarantee to do it, and no nonsense. Mind you, I charge £25 to do it, but if the cure is expensive it is quick.

I am not saying, however, that all professionals are stupid and have no idea what they are talking about. Many of them do know a great deal about the game. What I am saying is that too many of them have become confused. Let me explain what I mean. Many golfers, as I have said earlier, go to one professional and then another (a bad thing to do anyway) and I will guarantee that each professional they go to tells them something different. If you are one of those merchants who do this you will know, straight away, what I mean.

All right. Some of these professionals may be right – I am not claiming to have found the secret of golf – but it is equally true to say that many of them are wrong. It seems to me that what some professionals try to do is to tell their pupils something different. Never mind if it is completely mad, as long as it is different. No wonder so many golfers have back trouble. It amazes me that some are not in wheel-chairs, the way they have been taught to swing a golf club.

I have always kept myself fit, I have prided myself on that, but if I swung a club as some of these professionals try to make people do it I would hardly be able to feed my chickens, never mind play golf. It would kill me. So if I could not do it, what chance has an ordinary man who works in an office all day and who is not as strong as I am? The only chance that will come his way is the chance to do himself a permanent injury.

Perhaps you think I am having you on? I can assure you that I am not. It is not a funny matter. That is why I want to hammer home to you that golf is not a complicated game. When these old chaps with cloth caps and knickerbockers played golf years ago, do you think they thought about 'shut face' and 'open face', 'forward press' and all the rest? Of course they did not. They had a natural, simple swing – it was the only thing they knew. And considering the equipment that they had to play with and the courses which they played on, they seem to have been very good golfers. I believe if we all got back to a simple way of playing golf it would be better for everybody concerned. Having said that, I am not saying that all these old chaps had perfect swings. What I am saying is that they had simple swings. Fortunately some of us know a lot more about the game now, and know that the simple swing of today is a lot different from the simple swing of sixty or seventy years ago.

Talking of simple swings, when you are hammering a nail into wood you don't stop and think about how you are going to swing the hammer. It comes naturally. That is the way with most things you do. When you are having a cup of tea or a beer you don't stop and think of the most stylish way to get the cup or glass to your lips. You do it in the simplest and most direct way.

I never knew this man Ernest Jones who was born in Kent and then went to America to become a big noise as a golf teacher, but I have read about him. He had this simple business all tied up. It is a pity that more people did not pay attention to him instead of becoming all mixed up. It makes me sick and tired to hear golfers – I will call them golfers although, heaven knows, that is being generous – talk about this and that just like parrots. Of course, they have no idea what they are talking about – they are simply repeating what some professional has told them, or repeating what has been in some newspaper or magazine by a famous tournament star who, perhaps, has no idea what he does anyway.

You're surprised at that? You need not be, for many fine tournament golfers, champions even, have won many honours and a large amount of money without ever thinking about how they did it. At least it can be said of them that they had a style which was natural to them and which worked for them. There is one thing they almost certainly had in common, a good grip. I shall have a good deal to say about the grip later on, because I regard it as the most important part of the golf game.

The simple way! That then is the theme of this book. It is because I feel that there is so much rubbish talked – and written – that I have decided to write this book. Everybody who knows me knows that I like helping people. I have always tried to do that in everything, and, golf being my life, I like to try to help people to enjoy their game more. Before I started this book I had a good look at many club golfers. Honestly, I was sorry for them. I suppose I watched a hundred or more closely, and really not more than ten of them, perhaps not even that, have any chance at all of playing any kind of half-decent game. I saw them fidgeting about, moving their hands backwards and forwards on the grip, shuffling about their feet as if they were going to do a sand dance, having practice swings during which they kept looking up to see if the clubface was open or shut (although probably they did not quite know which was which), and then trying to remember everything they had been told they had to do correctly. Sad it was, very sad.

The truth is that they need not have got themselves all worked up, and if everybody I saw, and all the others who have got into such a state that golf for them is a task not a pleasure, read this book, I say that it would make them enjoy themselves. In addition to that, their handicaps will come down.

I am not saying, of course, that every one of them will become a good player. I am not a magician. Golf is a mixture of skill, strength and temperament. For people who have only a little skill, not much strength and an uncertain temperament, I can only tell them what to do. The rest is up to them. The chances are that they will never be very good golfers, but they will be better golfers. In fact, they will be surprised at their improvement. They will also be surprised at the ease with which they can play shots. They will find that the ball will be going away better with a great deal less effort. And this goes for everybody in golf – from the worst player to the best. The more effortless the game seems to be, the better are the results.

If anybody, however, picks up this book hoping and expecting to find it full of 'gimmicks', then he is going to be disappointed. Golf was never intended to be a game in which people got all tied up in knots. It is a game in which you have to hit a stationary ball with a club made for the purpose. I say, 'hit a stationary ball'. I should have said, 'hit a stationary ball from behind'. For that is where many golfers make such a mistake. They do not hit the ball from behind. Can you imagine a man playing bowls taking the bowl and bringing it down somewhat from way above his head. Of course you can't. He takes his arm back and

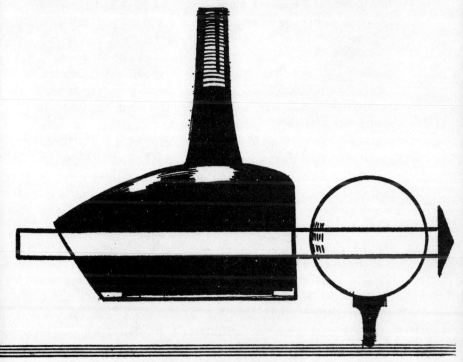

Attack the back of the ball

delivers the bowl with a low, smooth action. Many golfers can learn from this, for you never see a bowler send his bowl all over the place. 'Ah, but', someone will say, 'what about a bowler at cricket? He raises his arm above his head.' There is a simple answer to that – a bowler at cricket delivers the ball when he is on the move. In bowls the bowl is delivered when the player is stationary.

I instance this to drive home my point of simplicity. In many things that you do, the simple way is almost always the best way. And so it is with golf. I have been playing the game a good many years, and I do not mind admitting that there have been times when I have tried experiments. Nor do I say that I have always believed in the simple way. I wish that I had discovered it sooner when I was younger, for if I had I would have had more British Open Championships to tag on to my single one.

Now I am fifty-five years of age, and I think I play just about as well as any golfer in the world of the same age. I think I can say that, because my record in the Seniors' Championship proves it. I would not be able to play as well at my age had it not been for the fact that my game is simple and uncomplicated. So a simple method not only allows you to play better golf, it enables you to play better golf longer. And that cannot be bad, can it?

One last word before I go on into the whole thing properly and at more length. I know that when this book is published it will be criticised. There will be the golfing know-alls with their slick expressions who will dismiss it airily because it has no 'gimmicks'. There will also be the professionals who like to think that they, and they only, know how the game should be played. I am not claiming to be the first man to discover that golf is a simple game. What I do say is that I am one of the few who have been bold enough to say so.

If you read this book carefully and do what I tell you to do, you will improve your game. I cannot be more honest than that.

CHAPTER ONE

Getting to Grips

That girl (Julie Andrews is her name, isn't it?) has a record which says something about starting at the very beginning, and that's where I am going to start – at the very beginning, the grip, because the grip is important, very important, in fact the most important single factor in playing golf.

If you just stop and think for a minute about the game of golf, it does not take you long to realise that there is only one part of the body the club is in contact with, and that is the hands. I am not going to waste a lot of words and a lot of time trying to prove my point. There is no need to; it is a fact, and nobody can deny it.

When people talk about great teachers of golf most of the older ones at least will tell you that my great friend and old boss, Henry Cotton, is one of the best. In my view Henry has forgotten more about golf than most golf teachers have ever known. And Henry has always been a great 'hand' man. It was from him, I suppose, very early on, that I realised just how important the hands were. He was always stressing the point that the hands were delicate things, and the fingers especially so.

23

I once wrote about this, giving as an example taking a child's hand. Just think, when you are taking a child's hand, what you do. You do not grip it in your hand like a vice. If you did it would hurt the child. You hold it with your fingers gently but firmly enough to guide the child along.

And to use another example. Have you ever seen a blind person reading one of their braille books? The fingers fairly fly along the lines of raised characters, picking up each different outline quickly and transferring it to the brain. I can hardly think of any better example to prove just how sensitive the fingers can be. And that brings me to what I have to say next. That is that, while we talk generally about the hands in golf, we really should be talking about the fingers, although, of course, you cannot separate the hands from the fingers for they are part and parcel of the same thing. It is, however, the fingers which play the big part in the grip.

To stop any confusion I should say here that, when I talk about the grip, I am talking about the overlapping grip used by most golfers today. As many people know, there are many fine golfers who have used what is called the two-handed grip, and a few in the past who used what is called the interlocking grip. Dai Rees, one of the best of all British golfers, uses the two-handed grip, that is, the grip with which the club is held by both hands working independently of each other, so to speak. The hands are close together, but there is no overlapping of the little fingers of the right hand over the forefinger of the left hand, nor any intertwining of the little finger of the right hand with the forefinger of the left hand. The two-handed grip is used by golfers, and Dai Rees is one, who have fingers shorter than usual, and it works. Dai has proved that. But generally the overlapping grip is the one used and it is that I always think of when talking about the grip.

Whenever I go to a golf club and sometimes, too, when I am at a tournament, I see people on the tee putting the head of the club down on the ground, then putting their hands first

The Vardon overlapping grip

The two-handed baseball grip

this way and then that way on the shaft, trying, I suppose, to find what they consider the right grip. That always seems silly to me. If they have got themselves into such a state that they do not know the right way to hold the club, the chances are that they are not going to get it by experimenting on the first tee. It amuses me to see them open their left hand and lay the shaft of the club on it, then think again and lay the shaft on their hand in a different way, and then close their right hand on the shaft in one way and then another. It shows that they are all mixed up, and how can you play good golf shots when you are all mixed up in your mind? Sooner or later they are bound to wonder if they have got the right grip, or whether they should be doing something else.

I will try to make it all sound as simple as possible. In my opinion, when playing golf both hands are equally important, but let us start with the left. When you take the club, the first thing to do is to ensure that the forefinger and thumb of the left hand are tight together, tight enough to show you that the muscle – I have no idea of the name of it – at the base of the thumb is large. This indicates that you *are* holding the club with your fingers, and that it is not away back in the palm of the left hand.

If you are holding the club correctly, you will notice that the top of the shaft is hidden behind the left wrist and that the left hand is very much on top of the shaft. Now, you hear a great many people talking about the knuckles of the left hand. But, if you are holding the club the way that I have said, you want to forget the left knuckles. I have seen people look down at their knuckles, and then I have heard them say, 'I am showing two knuckles,' or 'three knuckles,' or whatever it was. When I looked down at the head of their club I noticed that the face was away as wide open as it could get. There was no way they could get it into the ball if they lived to be a hundred. I have already talked about golfers going into all kinds of antics to get their grip right, but what half of them have forgotten is to see that the head

27

of the club is correct. The face should be turned in, so much
turned in that they cannot see the face at all. Then, when
they have got the face that way, they hold the club in the
manner I have directed.

Never mind about the knuckles. That is very difficult to do,
this knuckle business, and just adds to the complications. Anyway, it is all so much nonsense. I should like them to show six
left-hand knuckles if they had them. In other words the left
hand should be as far over to the right as it is possible to get
it, as long as the thumb remains in the correct position. I suppose you will be saying that you would have to be double
jointed to do that. But that is not so. It is all a case of getting
accustomed to it, and in time it will feel very comfortable.
And, if you do hold the club the way that I have said, you
will never slice a ball, and all of you know that slicing
is the biggest bugbear that golfers have to contend with when
playing.

I cannot stress too much this left hand on top of the
shaft. It is very important. Remember that golf is a delicate
game. You are trying to guide the club – which, in itself,
is a delicate instrument as compared with, say, a sledgehammer. I know, because I have used a sledgehammer as
well, a lot of times. Using a sledgehammer is a brute force
sort of business, golf is not, although, heaven knows, there
are players who think it is. 'Brute strength and ignorance'
is an expression that has been used in connection with golf,
but that is all in my eye. A lot of nonsense, I call it!

So much for the left hand, then. What about the right
hand? Well, I am not concerned about that very much, as
long as it is as far over the top of the club as it will go. It
must not be under the shaft, always remember that. That is
a very bad fault. When you see the nails of the fingers of the
right hand when you are holding the club you can be sure that
the wrists are too far apart. And, when the wrists are too far
apart, what happens is that they get together at impact after
the swing has gathered momentum, and you will find that

the clubhead has turned right over. More often than not, you will have white paint on top of the clubhead where the name is, and I have no need to tell you there should never be white paint there unless you put it there on purpose. I have heard of golfers doing daft things, but never that.

In other words, the right wrist should be well over to the left. I know that I have said this before, but I cannot emphasise it enough. That is the way that Henry Cotton used to play, and there has never been a better striker of a golf ball than he was. If the wrists are together right from the start of the swing, you have control of the club. No last-minute adjustment is necessary just as you are trying to make contact with the ball. If the wrists are close together the face of the club will be flush to the ball, and that is what the game is all about – getting the face of the club flush to the ball at what is called 'impact'.

Of course, many other things can happen to prevent the face of the club from getting into the correct position, such as throwing the arms out or pulling the arms in. When you do these things the head of the club can finish anywhere. But we are not at the swing yet, and let me say, no matter how pretty your swing is, if your hands are not close together on top of the shaft you will never hit a golf ball correctly.

Now, when I read books on golf or articles on how to play golf, more often than not I read all about the 'V' formed between the thumb and the index finger of the right hand pointing to the right shoulder, and all that sort of stuff. This is all too difficult. If golfers start looking at the crack of their left hand and then the crack of their right hand, they are well on the way to becoming mesmerised. I think it is all wrong.

But if they want to talk about the Vs, then the V formed between the thumb and index finger of the right hand should point to the right shoulder, and the V formed between the thumb and index finger of the left hand should point to the right hip. I expect that will shake a lot of people. All right, I know that I am exaggerating things a bit as far as the Harry Vardon grip is concerned. I will go further than that, and say I am exaggerating by a mile, but I have the average golfer, and the slicer in particular, very much in mind.

I am not forgetting those club golfers who have the interlocking grip, or the two-handed grip. If they keep the two hands as close together as they can get them and the hands as far on top of the club as they can get them, they cannot come to much harm. Where your little finger is makes no difference. I get tired of these professionals who mess about with small details like that, trying to blind their pupils with science. Science, my foot, the only thing they are doing is giving the poor golfer something else to think about and perhaps to worry about!

Far more important than where the little finger of the right hand is put, is where the top of the shaft is put, and I say that the only place for it is hidden behind the left wrist. In saying that, I am not suggesting that you should become a contortionist or a magician and put the shaft there, following up with getting the hands in position. If the hands are in the position I have been telling you to put them in, then the top of the shaft *will* be hidden behind the left wrist. It cannot be anywhere else.

You see, the hands must work together. They must be as one. It is nonsense to say 'golf is a left-handed game', or 'golf is a right-handed game'. It is neither. It is a two-handed game, and here I would like to pay tribute to these great fellows who unfortunately have only one arm and who still enjoy their golf. Some have lost their left arm through some accident, or perhaps in the war, some have lost their right, but I marvel at the way they have improvised and so manage to enjoy their game. Good luck to them. The amazing thing is how well some of them play.

But these men are in a class by themselves. If you have two good arms and two good hands, then you have to use them in golf. If you do not, then the chances are you are one of those players who are all over the place. And, believe me, there are an awful lot of them about.

You see, if you try to make golf a one-handed game, unless you improvise like these chaps with only one arm I have spoken about, you throw the club and the right elbow comes away from your side. If you ask anybody to hit with the right hand, he will hit from the right hip and the right elbow will fly away. That is for sure. And the result of that? He will slice the ball to glory. There is nothing else he can do. You might think that such an action would stop a slice, but it does not. You might think that, with the right elbow being away from the body, the result would be that the clubhead would come in from the top and produce a hook, if it produced anything. I am not asking you to try this kind of thing, just take my word for it. It will save you a lot of trouble.

The thing is that when golfers hit with the right hand – and you would be surprised how many do – with the upright swings that they have, all they do is to hit across the ball, and the harder they hit with the right hand the greater the slice they will manage to produce. There is no doubt at all, in my estimation, that the whole left side of the body is the most important in the correct hitting of a golf ball.

This brings me to this 'fashion', if you like to call it that, of wearing a left-hand glove. I should say that about ninety per cent of golfers wear a left-hand glove, and I will guarantee if you ask them why they do it they will not be able to tell you. The reason most of them do wear a left-hand glove is that they have seen other golfers do it. I have never worn a left-hand glove in my life, and in all these years I have never had one blister on my left hand. It could be, of course, that they have heard somewhere that golf is a left-handed game. Indeed, years ago it was thought to be so, but we know better now. We know that it is a two-handed game, so there is not a reason in the world why anybody should try to grip more tightly with one hand than with the other. All a left-hand glove does is to make you hang on more tightly with the left hand. What I cannot understand is why these golfers who use a left-hand glove do not use a right-hand glove as well. I have often asked golfers that, but none of them have been able to answer me. They use a left-hand glove to get a good grip with their left hand so why the Hell do they not use a right-hand glove as well?

As I say, I have never worn a left-hand glove, Bobby Locke has never worn one, Peter Thompson has never worn one, and we have won a few championships and other events between us. Why then should club golfers bother about them? Do you suppose that Jack Nicklaus, Arnold Palmer and Tony Jacklin would have never won anything had they not worn left-hand gloves? Of course they would, because they are great golfers. Perhaps they would be even greater if they did not wear left-hand gloves. I certainly do not think they are great because they do. This left-hand glove business is all a lot of nonsense in my opinion. Until Tony Jacklin plays a round with a left-hand glove and a round without one and scores two or three strokes more with the glove, then I stick to my point. I know there are people who make their living, or part of it, producing left-hand gloves. That is fine for them, but the whole thing is that you do not grip the golf club tightly anyway, so why should there be any outside aids to try to help you to do that?

Look at it another way. The grip of a golf club gets thicker as it nears the top. This is another thing that I fail to understand. Here again is the old idea of gripping more tightly with the left hand coming into things. Why do they make clubs like that? I will tell you why. Because they have always made them like that, and the people who buy clubs have no other alternative but to use such clubs. Unless, of course, they take the trouble of taking the grips off, or rather having them taken off and put on again without any padding at the top.

I have often asked professionals why they use clubs with grips which are thicker at the top, and not one of them has been able to answer me. I am not saying they are so stupid as not to know that golf is a two-handed game. They do know that, yet they go on and on with modern grips. You would have thought they would have tumbled to it before now, but it appears they have not, because, I fancy, they have never thought seriously about it. All I say is that it is time some of them did. The grips on all my clubs are the same thickness the whole way up. I see to that. With ordinary grips I really do often wonder why golfers do not use right-hand gloves to equalise the thickness of the grips at the top. It would make a lot more sense to me. I bet you if someone had thought of wearing a right-hand glove before someone thought of wearing a left-hand one you would find that all golfers would now be doing so. Crazy, I call it.

When I am teaching people, and tell them what I have been saying in this book about getting the left hand correct, they often tell me that when they put the right hand, or rather the fingers of the right hand, on the club it feels uncomfortable because there does not seem enough to get a grip on. That is because the grip towards the foot is so narrow compared to what it is at the top. I am afraid, though, that I am a lone voice crying in the wilderness, and that golf club-makers will continue to make golf clubs as they have made them for years.

The only difference about the way they make golf clubs now is that, years ago, they made clubs to suit club golfers – as they thought. Now many of the sets on the market are what they call 'autographed' clubs. That is, clubs bearing the signature of some famous golfer who, having his name on them, plays with the clubs in tournaments. That being so, he designs the clubs to suit himself. The idea is that golfers will flock to buy such clubs either because they want to show them to their friends or because they feel, deep down, that they can play with exactly the same kind of clubs as used by some champion or other.

What rot! How can a man of, say, forty years of age or more who works in an office, who plays golf once a week and has about as much strength as a girl of sixteen, possibly use the same kind of clubs as are used by a very fit man who plays golf every day of the week? It makes no kind of sense to me. Does it make sense to you?

Another thing, most of the clubs ordinary golfers play with nowadays are far too heavy for them, and that is why they often grip the club so badly. One way of knowing that you are gripping the club badly is that blisters will soon appear, especially on the right thumb. If you find blisters there, or indeed anywhere, you can be sure that you are not holding the club correctly. The right thumb should be on top of the club, not at the side of it. You will get some fine old blisters if you have the thumb at the side of the shaft, I can tell you. In this matter, I cannot think of a modern professional who holds the club more correctly than Neil Coles. As near perfect as makes no difference, Neil is. If you ever get close enough to him to see his grip, you will find both his hands are so far over the top of the club that the shaft appears from under the left-hand side of his left wrist. That is perfect.

I have talked about contortionists and magicians, and this is what you may think I am asking you to become. Not at all. I am not saying you will take to it in a flash, not after years of gripping or holding the club any old way with, perhaps, the hands wide apart and the right one away as far under as you can get it. No! You may find my way a bit uncomfortable at first, but persevere with it for a little. If you have not got a club handy, swish away with a stick for half an hour at a time, and I will wager that soon you will feel quite comfortable. More than that, after a time it will be not only comfortable but natural as well.

I have sometimes heard that, if you are holding a golf club correctly, it is rather the same as squeezing a tennis ball, and that is not a bad description really. You see, that comes back to my idea that the fingers are delicate and sensitive. That being so, you are really squeezing the grip of the club rather than gripping it. I know 'grip' is the word in general use, and there is nothing wrong with that as long as nobody gets the wrong impression, and holds on to the club like grim death. If you do that, we are getting to the brute force and ignorance business. And that leads you nowhere except, perhaps, to Highland Games as a hammer thrower. In fact 'hammer thrower' is a description I have often heard used of a golfer. And, believe me, it is not a complimentary description.

There is another thing about this finger grip. You do not have to think about tightening your grip as you take the club back. I know many golfers are very conscious of the fact that their grip on the club should be tight when the clubhead is at the moment of impact. This is because the grip is not right in the first place. As the club goes back, therefore, they get into a panic and say to themselves, or rather think to themselves 'I have got to tighten my grip'. Now, there is a complication for you. When they are trying to bring the face of the club flush to the ball they are thinking about tightening their grip. I ask you!

With the grip I have been explaining, with the hands on top of the club and as close together as they can be, with the fingers squeezing the shaft of the club helped by the right thumb on top, and the top of the club appearing from under the left side of the left wrist, you do not have to trouble about tightening the grip. It will do so automatically. This is because, as you take the club back, there is added weight which you have to take. When you get to the top you are fairly firm, and when you are coming down you are getting tighter all the time. When you are actually hitting the ball you are gripping tighter still – all this happens automatically. The trouble is so many people try to force things, and that is where they go wrong. If your grip is right at the start, everything will go as you want it to go, providing that you bring down the clubhead at speed. But I will have more to say about that when we come to the section on the swing. Do you know the only time when I am gripping the club really tightly? At the very top of the follow-through, when the stroke has been completed. You have to be holding the club tightly then, or it might fly out of your hand. Not that that would matter, perhaps, if there was nobody around, but if there were people about you might do one of them an injury and, besides, you would look a bit of a B.F.

But, seriously, if the grip on the club was so slack at the end of the swing, so slack as to cause the club to fly out of your hand, you can bet your boots that it has been becoming loose a long time before that – for, after all, it does not take even the worst golfer very long to swing a golf club.

The ideal grip is one which makes you guide the club with automatic, increasing force. I know there are people who have said, 'Let the clubhead do the work'. What rubbish! The clubhead will not do any work on its own. You have to make it do the work. You will notice that I have said, 'make it,' and not 'force it'. There is a big difference, because, in golf, your grip is for holding and guiding the club. That is all.

'That is all?' I can hear some people say. 'There must be more to it than that. What about the pronating of the wrists, for instance?' Forget it, I say. If you are gripping the club correctly you have no need to worry about all these things you have read, or been told about. Anyway, half of them are just written or said to make the game more complicated. Just because the grip is the most important department of golf, there is no reason to think it is something so unfathomable that it has to be wrapped up in all manner of expressions that do not mean a thing. I can tell any golfer how to hold the club correctly very quickly. My charges are not made according to the time I spend with a pupil. My charges are made according to what I tell him. You can improve a golfer's game and give him lasting enjoyment in a few minutes. Surely that is worth more than giving him lesson after lesson and charging so much for each hour.

I fear that many golf teachers, in trying to correct a bad grip, teach their pupils hip movements, knee action and the like. They know that the face of the club is opening on the way back. That is why there is so much of this hip movement and knee action business. It is merely trying to correct a fault with something else, not necessarily another fault but, at any rate, something which is not relative. Mind you, for some curious reason, the ordinary club golfers hate to have their grip altered. They do not seem to mind having alterations to other parts of their golf but, to many, the grip seems to be something sacred.

That, and also because so many golf professionals hate altering something as fundamental as the grip, may be the reason that the pros try some other things first. I, for one, do not blame them for that. I hate altering a pupil's grip, but so many of them have bad grips that it just has to be done, for with a bad grip you cannot hit the ball straight, not consistently straight, anyway.

I would say that ninety per cent of bad golfers are bad golfers because they have a faulty grip, and not because, say, they have a bad stance or bad hip movement. The game I teach with its grip and low backswing does not depend on hip movement. It *creates* the proper hip movement.

If anybody told me to keep my hips out of the way, I would be lost, I just could not do it. If, during your swing, you have to think of one particular point like that your whole swing goes to pieces. It must do. But, if you get your grip right, and then get the arc of your swing right (and I will have something to say about that presently), your whole swing falls into place without your having to do any messing about thinking about this and that.

But I am getting ahead of myself, because, although I have said a good deal about what, in my opinion, is the correct way to hold the club, there are several other things about the grip to be cleared up. For instance, there is the distance the left hand should be from the top of the shaft. This ought to be simple enough, but it seems to trouble a great many golfers. I fancy there is a feeling that you get greater accuracy when you hold the club further down the shaft. I suppose this impression has got around because of the fact that many people can grip the short irons like this and produce accurate shots.

The ideal grip is when you turn your hands round and see an inch of club sticking out. Some people say half an inch is enough, but I prefer an inch, as that makes certain that the end of the shaft is quite clear of the muscle at the left-hand side of the base of the hand. You would be surprised how many golfers damage their hands with the end of their club.

I am not saying that you cannot get results by holding, say, the driver further down. You can get results, and you can hit the ball a surprising distance, but in order to do that you have to alter your stance and put the ball further back towards the right foot and play the shot like a spoon or a No. 3 iron. Of course people resort to that kind of thing because their driving has gone to pot, and it has gone to pot because their grip has gone sour on them. So we come back to the old story of trying to correct a fault with something else. Why not correct the fault the simple straightforward way – by seeing that the grip is right, and not go messing about with the stance? Remember, not only does the ball have to be further back, but you have to stand nearer the ball as well. The only time I would advocate going down the shaft is when the driving goes wrong and you want to employ a makeshift cure for the rest of the round. But really, you cannot go very far down the shaft these days, for in most sets of clubs the grips are quite short, certainly much shorter than they used to be.

The best cure whenever something goes wrong with the way I am now telling you to hold the club is to check that you really are doing everything that I am telling you to do. It is no good going to a professional, because, more likely than not, he will start mucking it about. You see, most professionals hate this grip of mine. A few even say it causes hooking. My answer to that is that you only get low-handicap golfers hooking. There are exceptions, of course, but in the main, long-handicap players do not hook a ball. They slice it. Slicing is the bugbear of long-handicap golfers, and every pro knows it, even though he might not admit it. Club golfers cannot be other than slicers, with the upright swings that they are taught nowadays.

Perhaps golf professionals are not fond of the hands being on top of the shaft because they are afraid of their pupils smothering the ball. That could be the reason why they are against my type of grip. But to call it a hooker's grip is nonsense. When you see the nails of the fingers of your right hand then you have a hooker's grip and you are in trouble, real trouble. But you will not get into trouble if you use the grip I have prescribed for you.

I am not saying that it will never go wrong. Of course it will, because we are all human and, that being so, you will not be able to do the same thing every time. If we could do that we would all be perfect, and no person is perfect, we are always being told, and it is certainly true to say that no golfer is perfect. If he were, he would win every competition he entered. The human element must always come into the scheme of things, so from time to time, without knowing it, you will depart from the grip that I have been telling you about, and you will find that everything will go wrong.

It is bound to happen, and the only thing that you can do is to start all over again. For heaven's sake fight against any tendency to start experimenting. More good golfers have been made bad ones by trying this method and that method than by any other fault. Half of them have no idea what they are trying to do anyway. All they want to do is something different. Such golfers have no more chance of becoming good than I have of walking on the moon. Not that I would not like to do that, but I will never have the chance.

I am an old-timer at this golf business, and during my lifetime I have made mistakes, a lot of mistakes. But, if I had known everything about the grip that I know now, I would have won more Open Championships and a lot more tournaments. However, that is all in the past. You cannot put back the clock, and now I want to impart all I have found out about golf to others. And let me say that much of what I have found out has been made clear to me in the past few years, when I have had time to sit down and think about the game of golf and work things out for myself.

Nowadays a professional has just to win a tournament and the next thing you know is that he has written a book telling others how to play golf. A load of old rubbish, I say. How can a mere boy, or even a young man, know what the fundamentals of the game are all about when all he is interested in is winning a big cheque? But then, some of these tournament professionals never even see what they are supposed to have written.

What I say in this book I believe to be true because I have found out it has worked for me. I have also studied thousands of words that have been written about golf and, more particularly, what has been written about the grip. Then I have weighed all those words up against my simple method of having the hands on top and the end of the shaft appearing from underneath the left-hand side of the left wrist, and my conclusion has always been the same. My method is the correct one. Not only that, it is the key to the whole game of golf. Forget all the clever Dicks who talk about the hips, the knees, pronating the wrists and so forth. If you follow their advice you will still end up by being a bad golfer, and perhaps a mental wreck into the bargain.

And that is not why you play golf. You play it to enjoy it, and if you can improve at it, then so much the better. I challenge anybody in this whole wide world to say that I have not always been, and still am, a happy golfer. Of course I am a happy golfer. But let me tell you this. If I had known years ago what I know now, I would have been a happier one.

So much for the grip, then. Now we move on to the next stage.

CHAPTER TWO

The Stance

Although I have said that the grip is the most important part of the game, it is not the only part. Mind you, I have seen one or two of us larking about and going up to the ball and hitting it without taking up any stance or giving any thought to anything but hitting the ball. Some pros, and I am talking about pros, are very good at doing this because they are accustomed to hitting the ball automatically, and because most of them have a good grip. But walking forward two or three yards and having a swipe at the ball is hardly to be recommended. All right for a bit of fun once in a while, but that is all.

Of course stance is important. It must be, when, just as your hands are the only parts of the body in contact with the club, your feet are the only parts of the body in contact with the ground. They are your anchor, in other words, and you would hardly get results if you jumped up with both feet off the ground and tried to hit the ball. Apart from anything else, you would have to be an acrobat or one of these dancers you see on television, the 'Young Generation', or whatever you call them. You know the ones I mean, jumping

41

about all over the place as if they had ants in their pants.

But, here again with the stance, today you are told to do the same thing that people were told fifty years ago. Never mind that equipment is very different from what it was then, or that we have learned a bit more about golf. Nobody seems to have thought about that, so we have the same old instruction trotted out. 'Stand with the ball opposite the left heel for the driver and gradually stand in a way which puts the ball progressively nearer the centre of the stance, or between the feet, whichever way you want it, and then have it even nearer the right foot for the shorter clubs.'

So here you have something else to think about. And, by this time, you will have gathered that I feel that the less you have to think about in golf the better you will play it. I say that every shot should be played with the ball in the centre position, that is, with the ball halfway between the feet. The only exception is if you are driving and tee the ball up very high. Then, with the swing I recommend, a swing which is very low, you can have the ball opposite the left heel. That is for the driver only. That is the only conventional shot in the bag which is different, because the ball is off the ground for almost the whole length of its journey.

Now for all the other clubs – the woods, the Nos. 2, 3 and 4, and all the irons right down to the pitching clubs. As the clubs get shorter you move just a little nearer the ball. You must do that, there is nothing else you can do. This idea of the shaft being in a diagonal line is much too difficult, in my view. Look at it this way. Your hands form with the arms the apex of a triangle. The club should be a continuation of the apex. That is the natural position. Why then have your apex and the club shaft at a different angle, perhaps not much of an angle, but at an angle all the same? The shaft straight out in front of you is right, exactly right, except, as I have said, when you are using your driver from a high tee, and for some other unconventional shots. Then it should be about two inches to the left, no more. This is to counteract the effect of having the ball teed well clear of the ground. I stress this high tee business because, with modern, deep-faced clubs, you have to tee the ball up.

No, this business of changing the position of the ball is far too difficult. It would take a very clever man to get the ball into the exact position each time. Heavens, every golfer would have to use a tape measure, and how he could use that and still stand in the right position I just would not know. Again, he would need to be an acrobat, and I am not being funny either. Surely it is much easier to look straight down the shaft at the ball. I defy anybody to say that it makes golf easier if you look down and find that the club shaft is slightly off straight by reason of the club being held in a diagonal position. It stands to reason that must cause complications.

My idea of a correct stance is that you stand to attention, and when you look over your left shoulder you should see the pin, always supposing, of course, that the pin is not hidden by the contours of the ground. Then, if you look down, the ball should be straight down, not to the left or the right. Perhaps I could emphasise it by saying that, if you draw a line back from the pin to your eyes and then another line from your eyes down to the ball, the two lines should form a perfect right angle. I have just thought of that, and it is the best possible illustration of what I am saying. A right angle. That is just right.

Tradition – I suppose it must be tradition – has meant that this moving of the ball for each club is done just as a matter of habit, really. I cannot think of any other reason why it should be done. I used to do it myself because, when I was younger, and even after I was not so young, I did not know any better. I know that when I was playing tournament golf regularly I used to experiment. I suppose that there is hardly any tournament man alive who has had his experiments written up in the newspapers and golf magazines as much as I have had. I used to say to myself after reading about something I had done or said, 'The golf writers must be

43

short of a good story, for they've got Max in the headlines again'. And, if they could not find something I had done, or said, to write about, they wrote about the clothes I was wearing.

I had no objections. After all, I have been a professional golfer all my life and, if you are going to be a successful professional golfer, a bit of publicity does no harm, does it? Another reason why I think the golf writers have taken me as their subject so often is that I have always been honest with them. I know lots of professionals who, when they have done a bad round, have made every excuse under the sun. They had all the bad breaks, their ball was continually in a hole. When I do a bad score and am asked why by the golf writers I give the right answer: 'I played rubbish'. You cannot be more honest than that.

More often than not, it was after a round in which I played rubbish that I started experimenting. But in those earlier days I rarely, if ever, experimented with what I might call the basics of golf. After all, everybody else did the same things, so I suppose I felt that if I did something different my game would go to pieces altogether. It was only a few years ago that I began to study the game from start to finish. That was when I had time to watch more club golfers, and saw how complicated they were making the game.

You see, to professionals the game is not complicated. A good professional begins to do everything automatically. If he fails to do that he will never be a good professional. And that is not all, for a golf professional, if he is a tournament professional, lives in a vacuum. He knows about his own game (or perhaps I should say that most of them know about their own game, for there are some, a number of whom have become successful tournament players, who have never had the faintest idea of how they play). But not every tournament player knows and understands the game of golf as it is played by the average week-end golfer. I do not intend this as any reflection on tournament pros. If winning money in competitions is the way that they earn their living, then they have no reason to think about anything else. In fact, it would be a bad thing if they did.

As for golf professionals in general, most of them do not care to teach anything very different, probably because they are afraid of being laughed at. I think that must be the reason because, if they made a deep study of the game – and many have – they might well come up with a lot of very different answers. I know I came up with a lot of different answers when I started to think deeply about the game. I know that a lot of club golfers, thousands of them, carry out their own experiments, but the trouble is they have little or no idea of what they are trying to do. As a result, they are on dangerous ground, very dangerous ground. A least with my experiments I always knew what I was trying to do.

Some people, when they are reading this section of the book, may still be rather unsure as to why the ball should be nearer the left foot than the right when you are driving. So I will explain. When you use the driver and the ball is teed up you sweep the ball away. With the other clubs, when the ball is on the ground, you hit the ball off the ground. That is the difference between the driver and the other clubs. Where your weight is, and that is in the centre, you can always hit the ball. If you keep your weight back on the right leg too much, then what will happen is that you will hit the ground. Then again, if you move your hips across as so many people teach, your weight has gone past the ball so you will not get it up. You will hit the ground beyond the ball.

Now there is another thing we have to think about, and that is the width of the stance. For the No. 2 wood your stance should be the same width as the driver, because the length of the shafts of the driver and No. 2 wood is not much different. But usually the No. 3 wood, which I like to call the spoon, is often appreciably shorter, so you have to stand nearer the ball and, as this is not quite comfortable to some, it is quite in order to narrow the stance a little, keeping the ball always central between the feet. I know that here I am in fact saying, 'Don't do as I do, do as I tell you to do', because I still have a wide stance for the No. 3 wood. The reason for this is to stop my hips moving too much, because that is bad. A wide stance also gives me better balance. But remember that I am a tall man, and a short man just could not have a wide stance. For tall men I would say they should have the same width of stance as for the No. 2 wood.

One must remember, of course, that there are many club golfers who are afraid of using the No. 2 wood. They have no need to be really. It is all a matter of confidence. But, having said that, I realise that, no matter what I say, the No. 2 wood is not popular with many average golfers.

The width of the stance is something I feel that all golfers must work out for themselves to some extent. That must sound a bit vague, but when you stand up to the ball you must feel comfortable. And when you are, or are not, comfortable, is something that you have to decide for yourself. You have not got someone at your elbow all the time asking you, 'Are you comfortable?' In golf, as in life, you have to make decisions for yourself. The width of the stance is one of them. But to be comfortable you will find that, as the club range goes down, you will have to bring in your feet until you are playing niblick shots. By then your feet should be fairly close together, the reason being that, as the shafts become shorter, there is not the same need to pay quite so much attention to balance.

One thing which always seems a problem to golfers is how near you should stand to the ball in relation to your size. You get people who say that, if you are very tall, you should stand much further away from the ball. I just cannot see that. There should be no difference at all in the distance tall people and short people should stand from the ball. The only thing is that a tall man has to bend his knees a little. And remember, I said 'bend his knees'. The top part of the body should not be bent because, if he does that, the golfer's stomach is hidden out of the way and then he rolls his shoulders.

Also, when people talk about this difference of distance from the ball, they do not take into consideration the fact that the tall man's clubs are longer by about two inches. At least they should be, if he is very tall and has chosen the clubs which are right for him. My clubs are actually three inches longer than standard, and I am not as tall as some golfers. I do not have to bend over to reach the ball. But there is no doubt that many golfers are playing with clubs which are not the right length for them, for the simple reason that the range of clubs sold is so limited. In fact, as far as I can see, most ranges of clubs come in only two lengths, the maximum of which is about forty-three inches, and even if you are six feet six inches tall these are the clubs you have to play with. The ideal thing if you are very tall, or indeed very short, is to have clubs specially made for you, but that is not easy these days when almost everything is mass-produced.

I have mentioned about tall men standing with bent knees, but then everybody should have their knees slightly flexed, tall men more than others. The thorax should be upright, so that the weight should be on the heels, and not on the balls of the feet as everybody teaches. What is the good of the weight being on the balls of the feet? If it is there, then the chances are that you will fall forward, for the ball is in front of you and you are going to hit it away from you. Naturally there is a tendency to go after the ball, that is why the weight should be on the heels, and your behind sticking out helps to keep it there.

The fact that your weight is on your heels helps you to maintain a solid position. It is because many club golfers have the weight on the balls of the feet that they throw themselves off balance, and stagger about like a drunken man when they play a shot. This is just because they do not squat down, adopting a posture of rest, which means

Keep your body-weight on your heels

that the body is upright with knees bent so the weight must be on the heels. You then reach the club by pushing your fingers towards it. You do not reach the club by pushing your head or your shoulders at it, you reach it by pushing your arms and fingers straight down towards the ball. Again I will make mention of these hammer throwers at these Highland Games. When they are in the act of throwing the hammer they are right back on their heels. Of course they are. That is the only way to send away the hammer. It is the same with sending away a golf ball. Some of these stylist chaps say things about Arnold Palmer being back on his heels, but Palmer has won a lot of championships and that is more than some of his critics will ever do.

Then we have something else about the stance which causes a lot of doubts in some golfers' minds. That is whether they should stand with a closed stance, an open stance or a square stance. There has been an awful lot written about this. My answer is that, generally speaking, the stance should be a square one. I have already indicated this when I talked of the two lines at right angles to each other. Mind you, there are some players who, if they take the club back low with an open stance, will do all right because their tummy will be pointing ahead of the ball and their left shoulder will be pointing towards the left at the address. If they take the club back very low then they will find that the hips will do the right thing much more easily, with the result that they will follow through much further.

Golfers who use a closed stance like the one Bobby Locke has will find it hard to get everything working smoothly, at least with my swing. With a closed stance the tummy is pointing behind the ball and the left shoulder is pointing away to the right. They can get the club back low all right, but they find it impossible to hit through the ball. So I do not advocate a closed stance in any circumstances. An open stance in some circumstances, yes, but a closed stance, never.

There are some people who advocate that you should aim

to the right of the target or the left of the target. All that is
a lot of rot. You should aim for where you are trying to hit
the ball. It is the arc of the swing that decides where the
ball is going. Yet I am conscious that many pros tell their
pupils to take up a close stance and point to the right of the
target, and that the ball will finish up in the centre of the fairway. I have news for the pupils – and that is that, more than
likely, the ball will finish well off target for the simple reason
I have just explained – that they may be able to take the
club back correctly and get the clubhead down to the ball,
but they cannot get it more than two feet past it. Bobby
Locke could always do it, but Bobby Locke at the height
of his fame was a golfing genius. A genius, I say, and one
who could whip his wrists through with tremendous power.
Then he used to slither round with his club keeping very
low on the follow-through. Those who have seen him play
will remember that, when he finished his stroke, his club
finished somewhere round his shoulders. But, again, Bobby
Locke was a genius, and I doubt if we will ever see another
like him. No ordinary golfer could employ his tactics and get
away with them. I am sure of that.

There is no doubt in my mind that the square stance is very
safe. But there are many who will feel quite comfortable
with a slightly open stance, and will get good results from it,
providing – and this is the rub – they can keep the clubhead
very near the ground as they take it back. If they are unable
to do that, then I say that they can forget the open stance. It
will lead them into nothing but trouble. And when I say
the clubhead should be very near the ground, I mean that it
should be taken along the grass, touching your right hip
with your hands. Coming down, the tummy will be past the
strike of the ball before the hands. The hands are last to
come into the ball, so there is plenty of momentum to give
a good follow-through and, consequently, a longer ball. Everything will flow freely. If it were not for the fact that I know
many average golfers cannot, or will not, take the club-

head back low along the grass, I would recommend an open stance outright with no 'ifs and buts'. As it is, there is a choice, but if you choose the open stance then you must do as I tell you, about taking the club back. And with that I will leave the problem, for, you see, golf always has been, and always will be, an individual game.

In all this about the stance I have been talking about standing on level ground. But we know that all golf courses are not completely flat. If they were, we would think them very dull indeed, so we are often met with a situation where the ball is higher or lower than our feet. Obviously, then we have to make some adjustments about where we stand in relation to the ball. Let us take the case of when the ground is sloping away from you. Then we have to stand nearer the ball and employ an open stance. You do not take the club back along the grass. That is too dangerous, for the chances are that you might actually catch the grass. Then, too, on such shots you should aim left of the green because your more upright backswing and the contours of the ground will mean that the ball will fade on its own accord, as you might say, and it will fade without your trying any old tricks to make it fade. Shots off sloping ground are never easy, so do not be tempted to rush at them so that you will get them over quickly.

The next shot off sloping ground with which we are often faced is the shot where the ball is above the level of your feet. In other words, where the ground is sloping towards you. Here you must stand further away from the ball, a great deal further away from it, because the ball is so much nearer to your eyes, just as when the ground is sloping away from you the ball is further away from the eyes. This time you stand square, and now you do use the low take-back of the clubhead. And, just as in the previous case you aimed to the left, so this time do you have to aim to the right. Then the take-back of the clubhead is different from what it was last time because, for as I have said, you do take the clubhead

51

back very low in the way I teach. If you did not do that, you would feel very awkward, and perhaps catch the grass as you were coming down – which would mean that the clubhead would have come down where there was no ground, so to speak. Playing this kind of lie is a very good way to teach my new method of the low swing.

So we come to another sloping lie – the one where you have a downhill lie. This is another one that a lot of golfers fight shy of. For this shot the stance is a square one, and you must use a more lofted club than you would use for the same length of shot from level ground. When I say 'a lofted club', I mean a club with a good deal more loft. You must not run the risk of seeing the ball scurry along the ground after you have played this one. I am afraid that happens all too often, and not only to ordinary week-end golfers either. Then there is another thing about this kind of shot. You must have the club right back towards the right foot. In fact, I think it is the only time where I say that the ball should be in that position, certainly for fairway shots.

If the ball is in that position, then you can take the clubhead back low. If you tried that with the ball midway between your feet, taking back the clubhead low would be almost impossible. You would strike the ground as you were taking the club back, you see. Another thing you have to do for this one is to close the face of the iron clubs, the implements mostly used for this shot. The top of the blade must be squared to the hole, and not the bottom of the blade. Does it surprise you that there is a difference? If it does, then take out your No. 5 iron or your No. 6 iron and have a look at it. The great thing to avoid doing in this kind of shot is to hit the ground behind the ball. If you do that, the shot cannot be anything but disastrous, and, as often you have to play such shots for your second, one that runs along the ground like a frightened rabbit can ruin the hole. Without hesitation I would say this is the most difficult of all shots from sloping ground.

Which brings me to the remaining one, the one where you have an uphill lie. Somehow or other, this one does not seem to cause the same amount of trouble. A good player can take a driver for a long shot off a lie like that. I nearly always do. You can take the clubhead back, just skimming the grass, and then you can sweep it through up the bank without any trouble at all. Some people might sky the ball up in the air, but this is because they are not taking the clubhead back low. And, let me say, it is not a bad idea to practise driving by playing off a lie like this, because it will give anybody confidence – for the simple reason that the ball *has* to come off the ground if you swing the club the way I want you to swing it. I tell you, some people would get their shock of their lives at the result.

I have said something on the subject of the placing of the feet in relation to the ball. Now there is something else I have to say about the feet – that is I am a believer in having them placed with the toes in, pigeon toed, if you like. Then you can get your knees going back with the backswing, and the right knee coming towards the left knee when the club is being brought down. If you have your feet splayed out, you cannot do that. You find that the left knee goes outwards, which is very bad. You cannot bring it in when the toes are pointed outwards. And you cannot push the right knee in and get a thrust when the right toes are pointed outwards. The correct position is that the feet should be square, or pointing inwards. Then the knees come in to one another, the left into the right going back, and the right into left coming through. When you can do that, the balance is good.

It also seems to me that most club golfers stand with their legs too straight. They splay their feet out at ten-to-two, which means they cannot bring the right leg into the left, and that, in turn, means that they have to raise their left shoulder and that they will chop the ball. Then, again, when the legs are rigid, they have to bend their thorax and their body, so that their tummy has a big curve and their backs are bent right over, and this causes shoulder roll. They roll their shoulders on the backswing and they roll them on the downswing. That puts everything wrong. I do not mind the position of the ball so much as I mind the way people stand up to the ball. The knees should be slightly bent, but everything else should be straight, and the club should be reached by the finger tips, the arms and hands stretching right down towards the ball. The chin should be tucked under the left shoulder, and the ball should be looked at with the left eye. Mind you, you can look at the ball with both eyes, but that makes the range of vision too wide. Theoretically, the ball should be looked at as if the right eye was closed, just the opposite to firing a rifle.

Now, coming to another point, should the left shoulder be higher than the right when you are addressing the ball? I say the left shoulder should be high and the right one low. As long as it *is* low, and not back. In any case, the right shoulder should be lower than the left because the right hand is further down the shaft than the left hand. In fact, if the right shoulder is not lower than the left, then something has gone wrong somewhere. Too many people, for example, stand with square shoulders which are stooped forward.

We have decided, then, that the left shoulder is higher than the right, and that the chin should be tucked under that shoulder. The chin should stay in its position during the backswing, and on the downswing it stays where it is until the ball is hit and the right shoulder rises and pushes the chin away. There are some people who say that the chin never moves at all, but, if you pay close attention to films, T.V. series, and the like, you will see instantly that the chin does move – after the ball is struck.

And that, as I see it, completes what I feel are the more important aspects of the stance. The two main points are that the ball remains midway between the feet except on very few occasions, and that pointing the toes inwards gives a freedom of movement which you cannot get if your toes

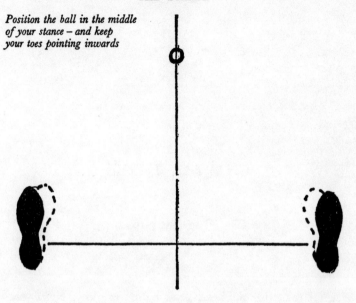

*Position the ball in the middle
of your stance – and keep
your toes pointing inwards*

are pointing outwards. The looking-down at the ball with
one eye is also important, as is the fact that you stand upright
and do not stoop. I feel sure that these and the other points
I have brought out about the stance will not only make you
feel comfortable, but also that they will make you play better
golf. Having said that, I shall now move on to the swing,
and tell you about the revolutionary method I have worked
out – a method I have, indeed, already touched on.

CHAPTER THREE

The Swing

When I take the clubhead back I am very low, but I teach people to be twice as low, for driving and fairway shots, that is, and you would be amazed at the difference in their game. First of all, they have to have the right grip. That goes without saying. But, if they have the right grip and swing the way I tell them to swing, I will reduce their handicap. I have had people come to me pleading with me to help them, and I have cut their handicap by half in one year. I am not joking. I swear I have done this, and all because I got them swinging low on the backswing. I suppose I am the only professional golfer who can say this, but the proof is these people I have told you about and, when I say that I have cut their handicap in half, I do not mean that they have had lesson after lesson. I have given them perhaps half-a-dozen lessons in a year, whenever I have been able to fit them in. You might say that, if I can only give them half-a-dozen lessons in a year, why do they not go to a professional who can give them a couple of lessons in a week. I am not going to answer that question, you can work it out for yourself.

The most important part of the backswing is the start of

it, and I repeat that what you have to do is to take the clubhead back almost on the grass, scraping the grass actually,
and that movement should continue for three feet with the
hands coming round the right hip. In fact, when I am swinging the club, I have the feeling that I am pulling the club
towards me with my hands, and the face of the club, after
three feet, should be pointing towards the hole. This is very
difficult to do if you grip the club the way many people grip
it. In fact, it is more than just difficult. It is impossible.

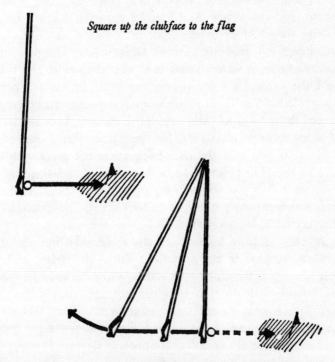

Square up the clubface to the flag

*Brush the grass with the clubhead on the first two feet of
the takeaway*

57

But my grip makes it easy to do. It is because my grip helps build up the rest of the game that I spent such a long time explaining it earlier on. I do not advocate a certain grip and leave it at that. My grip has its full part to play. It is not isolated. And I can assure you that it helps you to pull in the clubhead, and will ensure that the face of the club is facing the hole when it has been taken three feet back and is still near the ground.

I hear a great deal and read a great deal about the cocking of the wrists. You will not find anything about cocking the wrists in this book, except perhaps now, when I say that it is unnecessary. All cocking the wrists does is to open the face of the club. And when you open the face you have to pronate, or in other words roll, your wrists. That is what pronate means, roll the wrists. And you have to do that to correct having the clubface open. That, in my view, is out, and I will never tell anybody to cock their wrists. This teaching, unfortunately, is all too common all over the world, and it has held the game back for twenty-five years or more. That is since World War II. It is the worst thing that can be taught to a club member of over, say, ten handicap, because, when he tries to cock his wrists, he must make his swing more upright. If you take the club back along the grass with the face of the club pointing towards the hole, and then try to cock the wrists you will be very upright and the face of the club will be open. You might as well lift up the clubhead at the very start. No good at all!

When you have taken back the clubhead three feet the weakest part of the body at that point is the wrists, and, as you take back the club, your wrists will give, anyway. They are bound to do that. If they did not, they would hurt, so you do not need to tell them what to do. They will do it on their own, and at the correct time. So you have got it made. The face of the club is not open at the top. It is square, so you can forget about the rolling of the wrists. It is all past and done with without your knowing about it. They have given way of their own accord, and the hands have gone back and up without your fiddling about with them. If you do muck about with this pronating nonsense then you will not have a wide arc, and that is essential. The arc going back must be as wide as you can make it, then you bring the clubhead in towards the right shoulder. But you do not have to try to do this. It will happen automatically if you have swung the club low enough. The club must be nearer to you, so you draw it straight back to the ball. If the club has not been taken back low enough, everything will not be automatic. Then there could be trouble.

Now I can hear some golfers say 'But what about the length of the swing?' I do not think that is so important, but with my swing you *cannot* take the club too far back. It is impossible, completely impossible. You can bring the club back outside your right shoulder my way, and that is all. But if you cock your wrists then you can put your arms right round your neck. You might strangle yourself that way, but that is about all you will do. You will certainly never hit a golf ball properly.

That, incidentally, is why so many women are poor golfers. They have swings which are far too long because they cock their wrists, and are much too upright. I have taught a lot of women my golf method, and I have never had a failure yet, not one failure. It is sound, it is practical and it works with women just as it works with men. Why should it not? I will cut by half any woman golfer's handicap in a year, just as I have done with men's, providing, of course, that they are in double figures to start with. After all, I am a professional golfer, not a magician. You see, when they cock their wrists they open the face. Then they have to swish at the ball. Sometimes they can get away with it when they are in the mood, but it is no way to play good golf. That is golf by luck really, and under pressure it will break down.

So much for women, then. Let us get back to the swing proper. I have talked about coming in from the outside. That is the way Jacklin and other good players of today do it. But there is another way. If a golfer were to take the club back very, very low indeed, he would find it quite impossible to get the clubhead out any further than the right arc. He would also find it absolutely impossible to slice the ball. The best examples of this kind of swing I have ever known were Fred Daly, Harry Bradshaw and Bobby Locke – golfers who hardly ever sliced a ball in their lives. They were so low that they had an outward loop. But they did not get outside the proper arc coming down. They had no time to do that the way the more upright swingers do, so they brought the club down dead right, just in the same way as those who are not so low bring their clubhead down. Two different methods, one with an inward loop and one with an outward loop, coming down the same way and thus each achieving the same object.

For club members, I say take the club back low, very low. It is the safer method of the two because, if you are low enough, everything *will* happen automatically. It must do. There is no need to try to bring the clubhead down properly. It will happen. If it does not happen, then the club is not being taken back low enough. You cannot make a club come down correctly if you are wrong at the top. And you should be right at the top with my two grooves – the two ways of taking the club back – which should both be low, with many better golfers fancying the one which is not quite as low as the other. The choice is theirs, although I prefer the very low one. But if they are not right, then they have to think of slapping the left heel down, pushing the knee forward towards the ball to get them behind it inside, and keeping the right elbow tucked into the side. That's the only thing these fellows who find it impossible to use my method can do to get behind the ball to hit it. But they have to think of a lot of things to do it.

There are some golfers who have said to me 'I couldn't swing a golf club like that. I'm too heavy and have too big a tummy.' 'Rot,' I reply. 'Weight and your tummy have nothing to do with it.' And I say here and now that, if a golfer wants to get his handicap down with my method, he can use it whether he is tall, thin, fat or anything else. Playing golf my way can be done by people of any size, shape or form, with long arms or with short arms. Look at Bobby Locke. He was big enough, wasn't he? And he was the lowest swinger I have ever seen. Then Fred Daly was a short man, and Harry Bradshaw wasn't exactly a walking skeleton. These three swung a club correctly, in my eyes, and not these high swingers who have to twist wrists and twist their bodies on the downswing in order to get the clubhead in the correct position to hit the ball. To take the club upright and come back down behind the ball is very difficult, almost impossible.

You get Jack Nicklaus taking the club back inside very high, but then Jack Nicklaus is a very gifted man and he brings the clubhead back down inside and gets right down behind the ball. Jack Nicklaus is a natural, and that is what golf is all about. If only these people with this fad and the next fad would leave the players alone.

Take playing hockey. Using a hockey stick is a perfectly natural kind of swing. You just turn your body as a matter of course. You don't try to move your hips. The trouble is that these upright swingers are taught to move their hips out of the way when the club is coming down so that they can get the clubhead behind the ball in order to hit it. But who can think of all these things? If they swung the club round, just turning the upper part of the body naturally, everything would come right. I never teach this hip turn business. It's terrifying.

Oh, I know lots of pros teach it. They also teach you to brace your left side and tell you to put a towel under your right arm. I tell you why they teach that – because they are all upright swingers, cocking their wrists. They have to teach all that to try to get things right. If they taught a natural swing more like a hockey swing, there would be no need for them to be so complex. Through the years people have forgotten that golf is a natural game, and that what you are trying to do is to swish the club through and hit a standing ball from behind. The ball has to be swung away, not slapped away.

Those who have written golf books must bear a large share of the blame, or at least a great number of them must. All most golf books do is to confuse the readers. You have to get somebody like Henry Cotton writing a book before you get some sense – he knows that you have to hit the ball from behind and that the hands are important. In my view the fingers and the hands are the most important thing, then the arms. The body will then follow as a natural course of events. The body is a mere detail – for if you have got the arc right, the body must do its part.

This brings me to transferring the weight. Some people go mad about this and it is all very confusing. You don't have to transfer any weight. It is an optical illusion. I know some people do it, and some great golfers, too, Christy O'Connor, for instance. He moves his weight backwards and forwards, but he's like Jack Nicklaus, a genius. What club member could copy that? Christy did it as a boy and will never alter. But that is not the way to teach members to swing. When I swing the club back my weight is in between my feet, and when I go forward my body has a curve, and it looks as if the hips are across. The weight does appear to go to the left foot, but as the hips are tilted behind the ball there is that much weight behind the ball. In fact you have got half the weight behind the ball and half in front of it, so your weight is between your feet. Where else can it be?

These fellows who roll their shoulders forward and are all over their left leg ahead of the ball looking back at it at impact have got their weight over; but they have got their weight at the thorax and their shoulders over as well, so that they have a built-in slice.

Another thing I hear a lot about is the braced left leg *and* left side. That will always make the weight go over, and they must have a slice. The weight must be evenly distributed until the ball is hit, then the left side turns and you turn away and swing through. Even then, at the top you should have a hollow in your back and your weight should still be where the ball was. The weight doesn't go forward at all. You hit the ball away from you.

You probably think I am overdoing this 'natural' business, but I am old enough to have seen and known many fine boy players who were good, very good. And what happened to them? Somebody started to give them hints or lessons, and that was it. They were ruined. I can name a dozen of them that this happened to, but I won't – it would be too painful to them to think over what they have missed just because some know-all, almost invariably an amateur, thought he would teach them something about style. Style, my foot! Let amateur golfers get on with their own game. As teachers, most of them don't know what they are talking about. If they did, they would be trying to win money in tournaments instead of working at an office desk. In saying that, I would like you to know I have many very good friends among the amateurs. You will never find a nicer man or a more effective golfer than Michael Bonallack, or a greater character than Joe Carr. Great chaps they are. They know what they are talking about. I don't mean men like them, I mean these people who stand on the sidelines and think they know everything. Half of them couldn't hit a cow over the back with a banjo, never mind hitting a golf ball correctly.

After all, when you are telling somebody what to do in golf, it is important, it is to the person you are telling, anyway. About eighteen years ago I gave two people a lesson which lasted twenty minutes. One was fifteen handicap, the other was twelve handicap. When I saw them a year later, the one of fifteen was down to six and so was the other one. That is why I am charging £25 for teaching people my low swing and how to have the ball halfway between the feet, not off their left toe or heel, and to have the club held properly. Surely my charge is not high when it puts a stop to golfers slicing. Don't forget, many golfers have twenty or thirty lessons from their pro and are no better at the end of it. I will bet my life on it – I can stop a slicer and make him happy. And, after all, happiness is priceless. All I have to do is to give him one lesson. True, I may have to look at him again in, say, six months, and then it will cost him a tenner.

Another thing you hear a lot about is forward press. That is only for very low handicap players. Players of over ten handicap should forget it, because they have no idea of what it means. Actually it means relaxing the right side before you take the club back. If a long-handicap golfer tried it he would press forward with his shoulders and not his finger tips. I am afraid most long-handicap players think that forward press means pressing their whole bodies forward. When they do that they will almost certainly open the face of the club, instead of having it slightly closed, when the ball is being hit.

We hear a lot about the follow-through and the finish of the swing. So much, in fact, that one would think that that is the most important part of the swing. It is not. If you are correct going back and you keep your right elbow tucked into the right side, you can hit as hard as you like. When you get used to it there is no limit as to how hard you can hit, because you will not slice. And you can come down as fast as you like as well. In point of fact, you can also go back as fast as you like, but with my low swing you will not be able to take it back fast, not like these wrist-cockers who lift the club up like lightning. And you will find it impossible to snatch my way, for you are swinging with your arms. Remember that, after the ball is struck, your hands should be a yard from your body – which they won't be with an upright swing, because, with that, your hands must be drawn nearer the body. But with my longer swing and its wider arc you have got to throw the clubhead out and sweep the ball away, and the hands will naturally follow through and finish high.

The hips are tilted behind the ball which in this photograph is shown
further forward owing to the camera angle

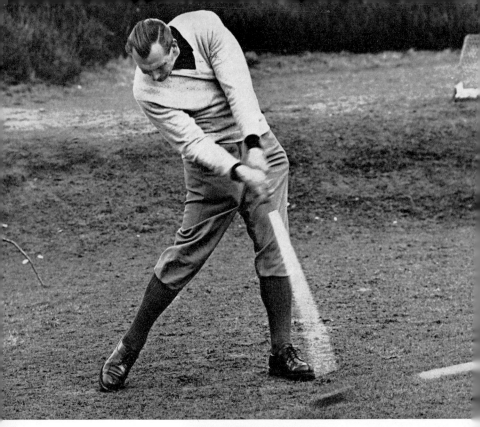

Max Faulkner at impact

Max Faulkner follows
through with a short iron

Swing easy – Hit with power

Now I will say something that is going to shock a lot of people. You can sweep iron shots away too, sweep them away without taking a divot. If I had my way, I would bar the taking of divots because we professionals do that only because of nervous reaction to make sure we get the ball. I do it, I punch down at it, but take a player like Ken Bousfield who has been pretty consistent through the years. He can sweep iron shots away, taking the minimum of divot. You see golfers taking divots the size of soup plates and, by doing that, they are expending a lot of force which would be better used in hitting the ball. If everybody hit the ball from behind, as I advocate, they would not be able to take a divot.

Sweep the ball away

Don't take a big divot

Another thing I do not place much importance on is what some people call 'style'. Golf in Britain has been held back a great deal because so much nonsense has been talked and written about style. The fellow who can keep his club low before he hits the ball and low after he hits it is the fellow who will play the best golf. Never mind about an upright swing, holding the hands high and all that sort of rot. Golfers who do that look pretty, but that's just about all.

It is useless, and under pressure it all breaks down, this twisting of their body. They look neat, but they don't hit a golf ball to hurt it. You can only hit a golf ball by swinging round your right hip and coming in from behind the ball, not by chopping down on it. Take some of the great American hitters. They are not high swingers. They may appear to be, but they never take the club above their shoulder and many of them are a great deal lower. Doug Sanders, for instance. It makes me laugh when I read the criticisms of his style. He is one man who hits the ball from behind and, even with his short swing, he hits it hard. How else can he get so much distance?

Again, I will repeat that one thing you have to watch when you swing the club low is that you have the ball further from you. You have to feel that you can't reach it because, if you swing low enough and are too near, you are going to swing right beyond it, then you will strike the ball with the heel of the club. But remember, in getting the ball further away from you, you do not bend your shoulders forward. A good tip is to stretch the arms out and address the ball with the toe of every club.

I will say this, however, ordinary golfers have to contend with the fact that golf clubs are not designed specifically for them, or at least very few are. Most modern clubs are far too upright, and this tends to make club players swing upright. In any case, most clubs have built-in slices because the faces are short and, as I say, too upright. If you lay an upright club on the ground you want to lift it up, thinking that is the only way you are going to get the ball off the ground. That's the way you get a slice. In my view, clubs should lie down on the ground, the same as they used to do years ago. If I were to design a set of clubs, I would design clubs which had flat soles.

I have talked about slicing and about clubs with a built-in slice, but people might say 'What about hooking?' Hooking is easy to cure. All hookers have to do is to move the ball back towards the right heel. I know this is against what I have been preaching but, if a golfer still manages in some way to roll his wrists, then he will hook. But it is not difficult to correct. Putting the ball further back will see him right at once. It is as easy as that. I am giving this hint to sort things out temporarily until he is gripping and swinging correctly again – gripping and swinging my way, that is.

Balance is important in swinging a golf club because good balance enables you to be most effective. When you have hit the ball and finished your swing you should have a hollow in your back, and it should be a natural hollow, if you have kept your head behind the ball and the eye still looking down where the ball has been or, in the case of a teeshot, where the tee peg should still be. If the head is in front of the spot where the ball has been, then the back will be straight and there will have been a tendency to push the shoulders forward.

I have said that balance is important if you want to get maximum effect. It is also important to safeguard the back. If you twist and turn all the ways there are, then you run the risk of damaging your back. That is why so many golfers suffer from back trouble. And it all starts with this business of taking the right hip back out of the way. People who do that get to the top with their upright swings and then, I believe, they are taught to move their left hip across, and that means their vertibrae are twisted sideways. They give them another twist at the top, and then when they come down and through they have to straighten again. Of course, some of them are going to hurt themselves. Besides all that, their balance is not going to be good.

Naturally the feet are important to balance, as I have said, and one thing I like to see is golfers on their toes when they hit the ball, or perhaps a split second after. You often see pictures of women golfers doing this because they have to depend on perfect timing, but you also find that some very good men golfers do this. It shows they are stretching for the ball. I never saw the great Joyce Wethered play, but there is little doubt she was the greatest woman golfer of all time, and from photographs she seems always to have been right up on her toes.

You come on to your toes because the left shoulder starts to stretch up towards the hole when you are coming down. The right shoulder then passes underneath it. Your right foot is turned in and the heel is off the ground long before impact. Mind you, there are some great players who can

A good swing is dependent on good balance —
A golfer who sways to the right is in trouble

69

keep their feet solidly on the ground and still hit the ball perfectly. Their natural balance is so good that they can do it, but I would not recommend it for club golfers.

It stands to reason that, if you are sweeping the ball away, your balance is going to be a lot better than when you chop down on the ball and snatch it away. A golf swing is not a thing of bits and pieces. It is one whole, co-ordinated movement with a wide arc, and the hands and arms all as in one piece when you are actually hitting the ball. Too many people try to do many things at the last minute and this is quite impossible. There is no time to do anything like that,

When you sway to the right it usually means you
are forced to hit off your back foot

so they are in a muddle and, of course, among other things their balance is wrong. Nobody can play any game successfully if they are off balance at the time of action.

You can't throw a cricket ball properly if you are off balance at the moment when the ball leaves your hand, nor can you throw a bowl correctly if you are off balance. You can't even kick a football as hard as you want to if you are off balance. Why then should you be able to hit a golf ball correctly when you are off balance? The answer is that it is impossible to do so.

And because your weight is still on your back foot on the follow-through, your shots will lack power

71

CHAPTER FOUR

Trouble Shots

I think it is true to say that some golfers have problems with certain kinds of strokes all their golfing lives, and so I will now deal with some of the really bad habits that can ruin, or at least spoil, the game for the long-handicap people. Let me start with fluffing. Good players very rarely do this, but the rabbits often do, that is why they are in the rabbit class.

Fluffing is caused by falling back on the right leg when you are hitting the ball. This, in turn, is because the club has been taken up too high above the head. This means that going back all the weight has been on the left side, and when this happens you have to transfer the weight to the other side to get the club down. The result is that the clubhead will strike the ground two or three inches behind the ball.

When you swing the club like this you are, in fact, doing exactly the opposite to what you should be doing as regards body movement. This is caused by the swing being far too upright. When you take the club back low your right side goes backwards, not sideways, and the weight is on the right heel. It cannot be anywhere else. That is what causes fluffing –

the weight being wrong both when taking the club back and when coming down.

Strangely enough, topping, which is another bugbear with long-handicap golfers, is also caused by the same thing – the weight being on the left side going back and the right side coming down. What they do is to keep back the weight so far that they top the ball instead of fluffing it. You cannot send a ball forward when the weight is not moving forward as well. It stands to reason you can't do it. I know there are a lot of people who try to bring in all manner of things as causing fluffing and topping, but the reasons are quite simple really, so simple, I suppose, that golfers think there must be more and very obscure reasons why they fluff or top. The reasons are not obscure at all.

Then there is the shot where golfers playing to a green skin the ball so that they get a flyer, meaning that the ball fails to rise and skims just above the ground, or on the ground, far past their target. This happens because the person playing the shot has been too wristy and has flicked at the ball.

There is no reason in the world to be wristy or to flick at the ball. The club should be low to the ground. For myself I use the ground as a guide. The ground is stationary so why not make it help you? Swing along the ground and the loft of the club will bring the ball up. You don't have to help the ball in the air. It is when you do that that the trouble starts. Because you flick at the ball the chances are you will hit the ball with the sole of the club and shoot it across the green. There should be very little wrist action going back. The wrists will give anyway, of their own accord, and if the weight is right over the ball you will play a good shot.

I would rather see long-handicap players keeping their arms more rigid when taking the club back for short shots. By doing that the arms and hands would at least all be in one piece when the ball is hit, and the ball would not go shooting along the ground. The trouble is that so many seem to think that playing short shots is an entirely different game from

73

playing long shots. And, of course, it is nothing of the kind.

You are standing nearer the ball. You must be, because the clubs are shorter, so you are playing from your lap more, say, from about four or five inches above the knees. You should be right over the ball, taking the club back round the right hip with the wrists giving naturally, then coming towards the ball along the ground, the swing being all in one piece. The length the club is taken back is a question for each individual golfer, but I see no reason for the club being taken back further than is necessary for the job on hand. It should not be a short swing because, if it is, the swing won't flow and it will be hurried. Let the club go back, and because you are not gripping tightly, you can take it back smoothly and in one movement. That is what is required for short shots, just as it is required for long shots. It's not a different game. Long shots, short shots – they all belong to the same game.

I often feel that it is this gripping lark, this having to grip the golf clubs with two hands, which causes a lot of trouble. But then a golf club is too heavy to lift off the ground with one hand. This might sound a daft thing to say, but I believe that you could get just as good results by playing shots near the green with your right hand only, for then the club would be coming in behind the ball and you wouldn't twist your wrists as many do with two hands. I suppose that one thing that you can do, if you are unable to hit pitch shots correctly, is to imagine that you are holding the club with your right hand. But I suppose that, too, might lead to complications.

To sum up the faults I have been dealing with: they are caused by steep swinging, wrong weight transference, cocking of the wrists and jerking at the ball. You see, even when I am playing a driver against the wind, I still swing low and have the ball further back towards the right foot with the face more shut, and hit the ball forward. With a low swing the ball cannot get up. You do not need an upright swing to keep the ball down, instead that will make it come up. And

I feel that most of the trouble with bad short shots is caused by the completely wrong understanding that many, many golfers have of how these shots should be played. They think that they are two different departments of golf, the long game and the short game.

If you pick up most golf books which set out to give instruction for beginners, you will often find there is a section for *The Short Game* and another for *The Long Game*. Why? They are not different sections of the game of golf, or at least I have never found them so. No matter whether you are playing off a tee or from any part of the fairway, golf is all one game, make no mistake about that. There have to be slight variations to meet certain conditions, that is all.

I suppose, too, that I have to say something about shanking. This is caused by the shaft of the club being flat and the wrists being high during the swing. Coming down it is soon clear that the clubhead is way out beyond the ball, but then there is no time to get it in the right position to hit the ball. The only way to make any contact with the ball, therefore, is to draw the clubhead in and across the ball. That is the reason for a shank, or at least the chief reason. The only way to cure a shank is to pull the hands into the side more than ever and then lift the club by cocking the wrists. 'Ah,' I can hear some of you say, 'What on earth is he talking about? He's been going on and on about not cocking the wrists and now here he is telling us to do it.'

My reply is that, trying to cure a shank, is the only time I would recommend cocking the wrists, because the shaft would go upwards and you have room to draw it down. Then you should try to hit your left toe with the head of the club as it comes down so that you are dragging it in. A shank is a low swing with the shaft of the club and a high swing with the hands, which is wrong, because what you want is a low swing with your hands and a high swing back with the head of the club.

Many people think that a shank is caused because of the

way you bring the club down. So it is, but the whole thing starts a good deal earlier than that, when the club is being taken back and an effort is being made to keep the shaft low. Because of that, the hands are high and the right elbow is tight in against the side. This usually happens with the shorter irons, from the No. 7 downwards. Now the club has to be brought down for the hit and the right elbow flies away from the side, which is wrong. If only players who do that could have a strap round their right elbow and round the waist they might do better, but then they cannot have that. There is no doubt that it is this right elbow moving away from the body which is one of the reasons for shanking. As I have said, when the clubhead is away outside the ball it has to be brought back, and so you hit the ball with the neck of the club and it shoots away to the right. Those who stand nearer the ball than they should are more prone to shanking than others who stand rather further away from it. Standing away from the ball is not a cure, but it might help.

But golfers playing little shots especially bring a whole load of trouble on themselves. You will see long-handicap golfers with nothing between them and the green trying to play all sorts of fancy shots. That state of mind has always been beyond me. What is wrong with a good old-fashioned pitch and run? Nothing. I play this kind of shot often. In fact I can let you into a secret. I have never used a wedge, not from the first day they came out. Certainly for the average player they are too heavy, and so the user is lost, completely lost. It is all right if you go to America where the ball will stop dead however low you hit it. But in Britain conditions are totally different and the greens much harder. So in my view, wedges are out.

When I am playing on a seaside links I often putt from thirty yards or, if I am a little further away, I might pitch and run, and for that I use a No. 5 or a No. 7 iron – not one of these great heavy wedges. Playing a wedge requires great accuracy, and I must say how much I admire some of the pros who play them so well. It is pretty to watch, but not for me. I imagine, too, that they practise a great deal. I think Christy O'Connor goes along with me on this, because I have seen him use a very light pitching club, perhaps a lady's, and he is just about as good at pitching as anybody you'll ever see. He just takes his hands back low round his right hip and the clubhead follows along the grass.

The trouble with so many players is that they don't think the loft of the club will make the ball rise. I tell you that, if you play a No. 4 iron for a pitch and run, the ball will rise, so it will with a No. 3 iron – and with a No. 3 or a No. 4 the ball will run more, which is ideal. But people will try to use lofted clubs, and they fluff and do all sorts of things. They never seem to learn. I do believe that many, indeed most, long-handicap golfers would score much better if they played more pitch-and-run shots, rather than try to ape the tournament pros. After all, the pros are playing golf for a living and know what they are about. But for club golfers to go out on a Saturday morning and attempt shots which are beyond them is sheer nonsense. It just shows that their mind is not on their game. Either that, or they feel it is beneath them to play pitch-and-run shots. Well, I can tell these people that these kinds of shots have won me a few pounds in my time.

There is no need to be afraid of running the ball along the ground when you intend it to go that way. I can tell you that there is less chance of making a mistake by doing that, than by trying to play a wedge, a club you are unable to handle properly anyway.

Now one big problem which faces all golfers, no matter how well or how badly they play, is getting out of long grass. Naturally, the worse a player is, the more chances he has of going into rough. Theoretically, playing my way, you should not go into rough, but I am not so stupid as to think that this won't happen, because, no matter what I say or anybody else says, the human element will come into the scheme of things. I suppose golf would be a dull game if that did not happen. So, when you go into long grass, what do you do about it?

Here I put myself up to be shot at because, playing my way, you cannot take the club back along the grass in the rough. It just won't go, so you have to do something else in this instance. What have you got to do then? The answer is that you have to hide the face of the club, pointing it right into the ground. I call it 'hooding' the face. You get the club back off your right toe and then straight up off the ground. I hate saying this, because people will try to do the same thing on the fairway – which is the very thing I am preaching against. I emphasise that what I am saying now is *only* for long grass, and nowhere else. You cannot take the club back along the grass, so you have to adopt another method.

Having got the club up, you then bring it in a downward blow with the face of the club closed, striking the ball first. I say 'striking the ball first' because you must not strike the grass before you strike the ball. In this way the club stops in the divot hole from where you have been digging out the ball. You do not have to follow through. You go up and down, and the shut face of the club which is still lofted, because you will be using a No. 8 or a No. 9 iron, will make the ball shoot up and go well out of the rough. A good thing for longer-handicap golfers to remember is that the main idea is to get the ball on the fairway.

Many golf courses have a great deal of heather on them, and I find that playing out of heather presents many problems for the average golfer because heather is very tough, and week-end golfers, not being all that strong in the hands, just cannot get the ball out. The method is just the same as for playing out of long grass. Again the club has to be taken up rather than back. But I stress again this is only for playing out of long grass and heather, *not on the fairways*.

So much for long grass. There are also many times when

your ball lies just off the fairway in what might be described as semi-rough. The longer-handicap players sometimes find a bit of trouble here because they do not have enough confidence, or perhaps not the skill, to play a long shot, so they are forced to take a very lofted club, thus losing a lot of distance. Now it is always wise to make certain of getting out of trouble of any kind, but from semi-rough it is a waste of a shot.

The secret here is to hit the ball first. You must do that and, if you do, then the ball will come out just as cleanly with a No. 3 or a No. 4 wood as with a No. 5 iron. But you must take your club up and bring it down without touching the grass. And again, I must emphasise that this is a different swing from the one that you use on the fairway because the grass is quite long and, if you try to sweep the ball away, the face of the club will strike the grass first, thus taking much of the power of the shot. This shot requires great precision, that is why the pros who are playing for their living are so good at it. They have to be, for a good shot out of semi-rough is a stroke saver.

Strangely enough, some club golfers are very good at this shot because they have an upright swing anyway, with a partiality to slicing. And this is just the right kind of shot for grass which is longer than the grass on the fairway. But, remember, most shots are played off the fairway and there you have to sweep the ball away and, what is more, you can sweep it away because there is no grass to hinder the clubhead as it goes through. So, I say, playing from longer grass and heather is a different kind of shot. To try to hit the ball off the fairway with an upright swing is just as bad as trying to hit the ball from the rough with a low swing.

I feel that many golfers go wrong getting out of long grass because they have the face of the club too open. It should be closed, because, even if the club is brought down sharply, the grass between the ball and the player will more than likely catch the neck of the club and wrap itself round it. This

79

will cause the face of the club to open. Many long-handicap golfers will not believe this. They think that the face of the club should be open giving them more loft. When that is done the chances are that the ball will shoot away to the right. I'm sure that has happened to you many a time, that is, if you are a long-handicap golfer.

There are times when the ball is teed up in the rough. Many people will say they never have luck like that. But that is not quite true. Everybody has a little bit of luck some time or another. When the ball is teed up you can safely use a wood if you are far enough from the green, and then you just play the shot as if you were on the fairway for the simple reason that there is no grass behind the ball to catch the club as you take it back or bring it down.

There are two things I would say about playing this kind of shot – that you should stand even more upright than you do playing from the fairway, and that you should stand a little further from the ball. You must make certain that you sweep the ball away, and that you do not come down on the ball. If you do, the club will go right underneath the ball, and it will just pop up in the air. Perhaps you do not have the confidence to play wood, although there is no reason in the world why you should not do so. Then, again, you might be too near the green to use a wooden club. So, if you think you should play a No. 3 or a No. 4 iron, do so by all means, but play the iron just like a driver and use the same low swing you would use on the fairway.

Mention of playing a shorter club just like a driver reminds me that my wooden clubs are all the same length. I have just never understood why the No. 2, or brassie, should be shorter than the driver, and the No. 3, or spoon, shorter than the No. 2. It can't be to help you to get the ball in the air, because the loft of the club will do that anyway. I can see some reason in making the length of the shafts of iron clubs different because of the snap you have to give some iron shots, but wooden clubs, no.

Now we come to playing against the wind, shots which cause a lot of trouble to the average golfer. The fact is that many golfers playing against the wind think they should alter the swing. This is all wrong. They should never alter their swing unless they are experts. Then, against the wind, the ball should be teed lower – that is, when driving, of course – and I always have the ball more towards my right foot. I look right down on the ball, in fact I play the same kind of a shot that I would play with a spoon, but with a driver. My swing is the same as I use with a driver, but not following through so much. The result is that the ball keeps down and goes no higher than a double-decker bus. If you have a full follow-through you will put the ball high in the air – which is just what you don't want. For fairway woods and iron shots the process is the same – hood the nose of the club, and see that the ball is back about an inch, or perhaps two inches, from its usual position. The swing is the same.

There is another fault that many long-handicap golfers have playing against the wind, in fact they do it with no wind at all, and that is skying the ball. Some people think that this happens because the stance is wrong. The stance has nothing to do with such shots. The ball is skied because the swing is too upright and the ball is slapped away with a steep, downward swing. The result is that the ball is hit with the top of the club. In other words, the club has gone underneath the ball. Golfers who swing my way will never do that. You might top the ball, but never sky it. If anybody skies the ball, thinking they are using my method, I say here and now that they are not using it. With my way the ball bores forward and runs after it lands; it does not go high in the air and then fall on the ground with a plop.

The whole thing is that so many golfers are afraid of playing in a wind, but their fear is nothing to the feeling of almost terror which strikes them when they go into a bunker. I am not going to say that going into sand is a pleasant experience, it is anything but. At the same time, however, there is no need to panic. The trouble is that most players have no real idea of what they should do when they get into a bunker. But before I suggest what they should do let me say that, in most cases, the club they use for getting out of sand is much too heavy, and that does them no good at all. You can punch out the ball with a heavy club, but you cannot swish it out.

When I play a bunker shot I 'frying pan' the shot, that is, use the club as if it were a big frying pan and sling it along the top of the sand with a low backswing. The club must have a flat face. If the one that you have is not· very flat, get the pro to alter it. Then you will be able to stand well away from the ball. The ball should be between the feet, and the stance very open – in fact you should be almost facing the hole. Then the ball can be swished away, and, remember this, the left hand should be the dominant hand. It is the *only* shot in golf where the grip with the left hand should be stronger than the grip with the right hand. You merely lay the right hand on the club, and you use what might be called a dragging action. When you have finished the stroke the face of the club should be pointing to your face. But, if the face of the club is pointing towards the sand or pointing to the left, then the shot has not been carried out properly and the ball will have gone into the bank of the bunker. Too many players use an upright stroke in a bunker, and I admit that the ball can be dug out of the sand that way, but the chances are it will land on the top of the bank, not even on the green, and far from the flag. Of course, if the ball is buried, then you have to dig it out. There is nothing else you can do.

Why people are terrified of bunkers is because they have a bad method which has failed them continuously. When I see a golfer go into a bunker and place his feet so that he is right over the ball I say to myself 'He's going to be damned lucky if he gets out'. If he takes plenty of sand he might well get the ball out, but that is just about all. You have to be

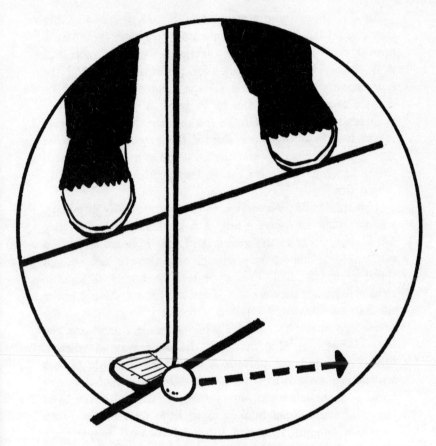

Open your stance and the club-face when in a bunker

a very good golfer to get out of a bunker that way. I know I find it hard, and for the average club player it is almost impossible. A good player can dig the ball out if he hits the sand about half an inch behind the ball, but great accuracy is required, very great accuracy. A strong left-hand grip, a strong left side and a frying-pan shot. That is what club men should do. Then they will get out of the sand. Not only that, they will also get the ball fairly near the hole.

83

Another thing about many golfers. Somehow they feel that they should take a bucketful of sand every time they play a bunker shot. I would say an eggcupful would be more like it if you are playing my way, or perhaps a cupful if the sand is very loose. That is all the sand which should be skidded away. And you can hit as hard as you like my way because the quicker the stroke the quicker the ball will stop. If the flag is at the other side of the green then play the shot a bit more slowly and the ball will run more. But it is the quick shot that gives the ball spin. Most golfers fail to realise this.

This spin business is foreign to the vast majority of golfers, whether they are playing out of a bunker or whether they are playing shots to the green. And that is because they do not strike the ball sharply enough and there is not enough speed under the ball. Pros appear to be hitting these little shots slowly, but they are not. They are hitting sharply under the ball and driving it forward. Even very short shots to the green have to be hit sharply, bringing the left hand and the left side into the shot in much the same way as when a bunker shot is being played. A good idea for little pitches and bunker shots is to wrap two or three fingers of the right hand over the left hand, thus taking the strength away from the right hand. Like bunker shots, little ones to the green require a different technique to straightforward, longer shots from the fairway.

I know a lot of people are going to disagree with me when I say, as I did earlier, that it is not necessary to take a big divot. You certainly do not stop the ball any more quickly by taking a big divot. That's for sure. In fact, if you hit the ball cleanly off the ground, you will stop it more quickly because you have imparted more speed to the ball and you can only get speed on the ball by coming into contact with it. But you have to choose the right club, and if you are near the green it stands to reason that the club must be a lofted one unless, of course, you are going to run the ball along the

Normally, the amount of sand taken in bunker shots should be no more than an eggcupful

ground. Many golfers would be far better doing that than trying to take a divot the size of a soup plate.

For club golfers taking divots should be barred, because they play a different way from professionals who do take divots after they hit the ball, and rely on the soft greens stopping it. That is why Bobby Locke, and lots of other pros – nearly all pros actually – are always advocating soft greens. And you have to remember, too, that pros have very strong hands and arms and, even when they take a divot after they hit the ball, they are still able to get a lot of speed on the ball.

Having said that, I will wager that if the professionals had no pressure on them they would not take any divots. I know myself that when I play practice rounds, or when I am playing in an exhibition match, I can go round without taking a single divot. Yet when I get into a tournament I am scared to play like that, I suppose because almost every other competitor is doing it. So I do the same as them. It's ridiculous really. Fright, that's all it is. If I only had the nerve to swish the ball off the ground without taking divots I should play and score a lot better. I used to do that, but I suppose as I have got older I haven't so much confidence now. Divot-taking is caused by pressure, nothing else. And just think, if there was no divot-taking, how much better golf courses would be. You have only to see a golf course after a big tournament to realise the damage that has been done. It looks as if somebody has been digging it up with a spade. Every fairway is pitted with holes where divots have been taken out, and perhaps have either not been replaced, or have been carried away by crows.

CHAPTER FIVE

Putting

I have touched on several departments of the game that trouble golfers, but it is true to say that putting is the most troublesome department of all. A missed putt of a foot is a stroke just the same as a drive of three hundred yards and, that being so, a missed short putt is the most frustrating experience in the game. The 'jerks', the 'twitters', the 'twitch' – they all happen to everybody on the green at some time or another, or, rather I should say, happen to everybody many times.

Golfers have been known to give up the game because of the sufferings they have had to bear while putting. New methods are tried, gimmicks are used and putters are changed. These help for a time, but usually things get as bad as ever again as golfers search for the secret. I have a lot of sympathy for them because I have done all these things myself through the years, as most people know. Mind you, some of the things that have been written about my putters and my putting styles have been built up to big stories from small stories. But I have never minded that.

Look what they have written about my clothes. 'Max – the

peacock', 'Faulkner looked like a couple of rainbows rolled into one', and all that kind of stuff. It's all good publicity, and anyway I like to wear bright clothes. They make me feel good and cheer me up at the same time. The colours of my clothes may not please everybody, but I defy anyone to say, 'Max Faulkner was badly dressed'. I hate slovenly-looking golfers, I always have done.

But it is putting we are on, not clothes. So I will get back to the subject. Is there a secret in putting? Yes, there is and it is now standing me in good stead. I shall explain it in a moment, but first let me say that most people when they putt are far too wristy. When you see a wristy putter you can bet he's not much good, for the face of the club is not square, not for one half inch of its path. The only way to putt is to be locked right through the arms down to the ball. The stance should be upright, at least it is better upright, but the main thing here is to be comfortable. However, the really important thing is that the movement has to come from the shoulders, and the movement has to be done from the shoulders all in one piece. That's point No. 1. No. 2 is that the backswing has to be longer than the follow-through. Gary Player is a good example, so is Jack Nicklaus, and so is Bobby Locke – and there will never be another putter like him, in my opinion.

The reason why you have to stop the through swing is that, if you do follow through, the putter has to come off the ground, that is commonsense. Follow-through putters three putt far more than those who do not follow through. I have the evidence of my own eyes to prove this. The reason is that, when they follow through, the ball is not always hit in the centre of the blade because the putter is already coming up. That being so, they hit the ball with the bottom of the blade. The result is that they finish five feet short. Next time, determined to be up, they hit the ball too hard and, if the putt is not straight, the ball goes whizzing past the hole. Bobby Locke told me years ago he took the putter back on the inside about two feet with no follow-through. By doing that he knew exactly just how far the ball was going.

Now, what I am saying is just the reverse of almost everything that has been said and written about putting. Not long ago I read an article which said that you should have a

*Bobby Locke – Always took the club back
on the inside when putting*

long follow-through in putting. I only hope all the professionals do that because, if they do, I shall still be winning money when I am sixty. It is strange that, while we have some good putters like Coles and Huggett, most British pros have not yet got the message, despite the fact that they now see so many Americans, hardly any of whom follow through. And as for club players in Britain! I can only surmise nobody has ever told them how to putt properly.

No follow-through, that's the secret of good putting. Oh, of course, those putters who follow through hole putts sometimes, but they miss an awful lot under pressure because, in their anxiety, they let the putter come up earlier and the ball is left short, or, if the ball is hit with the middle of the putter, following through the ball goes miles past. It is as simple as that. The only other thing I would say is that the head should be over the ball.

Naturally there is a bit more in putting than the right way of striking the ball. For instance, there is the reading of greens. Most players are bad at that. One thing you must do when you are reading a green is to have a look at the ground round the green. See how it slopes, and how the green slopes in relation to it. It is strange that very often most, or at least many, greens all slope the same way – to the sea, perhaps, or towards a landmark in the vicinity.

Having had a good look at the surrounds, then you have to have a good look at the undulations on the green. These fox you sometimes, but if you look at the hole from behind your ball and then from the other side, you should be able to make something of the borrow. If you are quite unable to see borrows on greens, and commonsense comes into this, then there is not much hope for you. But your eyes should be able to see the high part of a green and the low part, and then you must judge for yourself where to hit the ball so that it will drop into the hole. This is one part of golf that depends on the individual. And, talking about individuals, it does not really matter what type of putter you use; it makes no

Restrict your follow through when putting

difference at all. For myself I use a long-shafted putter
because I think that all clubs are too short anyway. A longer-
shafted putter will make you less inclined to wristiness, and
that is where all the trouble starts. If you are wristy you cannot get the club back far enough, the face of the club is open
when it strikes the ball, and the ball is also struck with the
club going up. It is this kind of putting which has caused so
much despondency to golfers, and if golfers continue to use
it the despondency will continue. No doubt about that.

I am not saying that 'one-piece' putting, with a smooth

91

and quite long backswing and no follow-through, will get the ball into the hole every time. Lack of concentration and the general failings of the human mind will see to that. But it is a sound method of putting, the soundest there is, and I maintain that it brings better results than any other method I know.

Many golfers have tried other methods and made them work because of the fact that putting is a very individual department of golf. I have made some very strange methods of putting work in my time, but, alas, not for long, for always something has gone wrong. With the method I have described there is less to go wrong. Therefore it must be sound, and have more chance to bring at least some kind of lasting success.

There are many golfers who go through their golfing life using the same putter. There are others – and I have been one of them – who use many different putters. Who is right? Nobody can tell, for it depends on each individual. Nowadays I suppose that the most popular putter is the centre shafted type. Some use an ordinary blade putter and a few of the older golfers use what is called the Mills type, which is an aluminium putter with a large head. Some use the shorter Trevillion type putter.

The great thing is to get a putter in which you have confidence, and for ordinary golfers I say that if you get a putter which you like, stick to it. Strange advice from me, perhaps, but now on looking back on my golfing career, perhaps I might have been better to have stuck to one or two implements. But for those who have to play golf for a living that is not easy. We have always to look for a way to score better, and if we have an off-spell in putting it is natural that we should try to find excuses, forgetting that it is the man at the end of the putter who makes the ball go into the hole, not the putter on its own.

It is very important that the putter is the right weight. I have always thought that a light putter is best, but there are those who say that a heavy putter on heavy greens is best.

But a golfer cannot very well carry two putters in his bag, so it is a case of striking a happy medium.

The length is the important factor, and in this direction each golfer must try to find the length which suits him best. Recently there has been a great campaign in Britain in favour of a split-handed method of putting publicised by the London artist Paul Trevillion. For short putts I am quite in favour of the two hands being apart. Holding a putter like that does away with wristiness, and if I had been younger I would have had a go at it myself, and I think I would have done well with it, for there is much to be said in its favour. But for short putts only, I fancy.

I really do not think that the type of putter is of any great importance, nor, perhaps, that how you hold the putter is of any great importance either. My point is that you should keep the blade of the putter near the ground, and keep the length of the stroke down to a minimum. In putting the thing that matters is getting the ball into the hole. Never mind if people think you look silly. As long as you are getting results, appearance matters nothing at all. And people will soon stop laughing if you are playing against them and you beat them.

There has been more nonsense talked and written about putting than about any other department of the game, and I suppose that will go on as long as golf is played. Get a good and sound method of hitting the ball, use your common-sense – and to Hell with what anyone says. Whether your putter is four feet long or is two feet long is of no importance as long as you put the ball out of sight more often than others, although personally I favour a long putter. And remember that, more often than not, towards the end of a round is the time when the pressure is on. That is when a good, simple way of putting comes in useful. My method is just that. Perhaps it will not work every time, but it will work better than a method which is more complicated.

When you have found a simple method and a putter in which you have confidence do not be afraid to spend hours

*Trevillion – Split-hand putting
exponent*

94

and hours on the putting green. Practising on the putting green is hardly the same as putting under pressure, but it does help to give you confidence. Do not think of putting as another and, perhaps the most important part of the game of golf. Just regard it as another essential part. It is because some golfers regard putting as the most important part of golf that they fall down on it so often. Of that I am quite sure. If you don't believe me just think of the number of times that you have seen professionals putting well when there was nothing at stake and, when it came to a big tournament, they missed putt after putt. And all because their nerves have gone to pieces, and an unsatisfactory method of putting was unable to take the strain.

CHAPTER SIX

More About Trouble

Now I shall go on to say something more fully about correcting common faults, or rather on the subject of correcting faults. If you play the way that I advise you to play all the time not many faults will creep into your game. In fact no faults at all should creep into your game. You don't make mistakes when you do simple things. You only make mistakes when you try to do something difficult. Everybody knows that.

But I also know that, human nature being what it is, golfers will get into bad habits on the golf course and they do so because they just do not think what they are trying to do. Then, when things get bad, they try everything they can think of, which only makes matters worse for the simple reason that there is only one way to correct what they are doing wrong. That is, by getting back to what I have told them to do.

I often have pupils who come to me and say 'I'm slicing', or 'I'm pulling', or something else. They then go on to tell me that they have tried this and that, and things are either no better, or that the very opposite to what they wanted to happen has happened.

Another shot showing
follow through with a
short iron

Address position for
short iron shot

Max Faulkner getting out of trouble

Max Faulkner on the putting green

'Right', I tell them. 'Come outside and play a few shots.'

When I see them I am horrified – completely horrified, for they have got as far away from playing the way I taught them to play as I am from walking on the moon. They were doing nothing right, and their game was in a terrible mess. In such cases I do not begin to give them a quick cure for the faults they have adopted. The only way I could do that would be to correct their faults with another fault, so what I do is to go over with them the basic principles of my grip and my swing, and tell them to get themselves sorted out on the practice ground. You would be amazed at the difference that makes, and before long they are as happy as a dog with two tails.

If you are not gripping and swinging correctly several things can happen. The first thing is that you might start to hook the ball, and more likely you will hook because your right hand has gone round under the shaft of the club. A 'hooker's grip', call that, and it is true. A hooker's grip very often goes hand-in-hand, or perhaps it should be hand-and-foot, with a closed stance – that is, a stance in which the left foot is further forward than the right foot. What usually happens is that it is the right hand which goes wrong first, and some golfers tell themselves that they must stand a bit differently, so they stand facing away to the right of the fairway.

More than likely they discover they cannot get the clubhead into the ball without turning their shoulders, so their swing gets flatter and flatter, and the more they try to get the ball to go to the right the more it keeps going to the left. An unorthodox substitute for an orthodox method is no substitute at all. That is why I am not going to recommend you to do this and that to give you a permanent cure. It would not be a permanent cure at all. But, having said that, I realise that when things go wrong they can go wrong suddenly, in the middle of a round. The reason they do go wrong is that what I preach has not been practised. However, things having gone wrong and a big hook having developed, check on your grip first. Ten to one the right hand has gone right under the shaft. Get it back on top as far on top as it will go.

Having checked the grip, have a look at your feet next. If you have closed your stance then it is certain that you will be turning your shoulders and also rolling your wrists. So keep the stance open if anything, take the club back low and, above all, do not hurry the swing. Hookers are notoriously quick swingers. I am sure you have heard the expression 'That was a quick hook'. These words mean exactly what they say.

Hooking mostly happens when a player is under pressure because, as I have hinted, the swing has quickened up. I do not rate hooking as quite as dangerous a fault as slicing because, on many, perhaps, most golf courses there is more trouble on the right than on the left and, besides, a ball which is hooked travels further. If the ball is hooked badly it also travels further into the rough, and that can be costly. But again hooking comes a little less often than slicing – which some people take a long time to get rid of.

The reasons for slicing are more or less the opposite, except that it is caused mostly by swinging the club wrongly. With my grip the hands are as far on top of the club as they can be, so the right hand cannot get any further over. It can be however, that the left hand has gone under the shaft a little, so check on that.

But we have to look at the swing to get at the real root of slicing. If the club is taken back on the inside and not on a wide arc, something has to be done to throw the clubhead out at the top of the swing to get it down behind the ball. Then, what usually happens, is that the clubhead is thrown too far out and has to be brought down across the ball. At the moment of impact the face of the club is not square to the ball. In fact, it is turning outwards, and it is that which causes the most almighty slice.

With my method you cannot slice, so if you are slicing you are not doing as I say. You must get the club back low and on a wide arc, with the arms well outstretched. Then the wrists will cock naturally and the clubhead will be brought down behind the ball. An open stance will accentuate a slice.

Now on to fluffing or as the older golfers used to call it 'scaffing'. This fault is rarely to be found among lower handicap golfers, but is certainly to be found among higher handicap players. This is when the ground behind the ball is hit. And there are two main reasons, the first that the left knee has been bent when the club is taken back, and the second that consequently on the bending of the left knee the weight has been put on the left foot. And this is just the opposite to what should happen.

The swing is all to pot because the bending of the left knee sees to that. The clubhead has to be thrown out, and the player usually thinks to himself that the weight has to be transferred, so he does just that. He transfers the weight to the right foot – again just the opposite to what he should do. But he cannot help himself because his left shoulder has dipped. Further to that, I can say little more about fluffing – except that when you fluff a shot you are wrong, all wrong.

The cure? It is to swing all in one piece and see to it that, when the club is taken back, the weight is not on the left foot. Remember, too, not to dip the left knee, for that causes you to swing more upright and everything becomes loose. Being loose and sloppy is the reason the clubhead is thrown out at the top of the swing.

Smothering is a somewhat similar shot. Smothering happens when the face of the club is turned in when the ball is hit, and the result is that the ball scuttles away along the ground like a ferret after vermin. A bad position at the top of the swing is the fault here. Many people are inclined to let go the club with the left hand when the club is at the top of the swing, and it is this looseness of the left hand when the club is at the top of the swing that plays the major role in smothering the ball. As in fluffing, the wrong transference of the weight can also cause a golfer to smother the ball, for the weight being on the right side when the club is being brought down means that there is no proper contact with the ball -- which goes away at a tangent and usually into very bad rough.

Many readers who have forgotten their earlier problems may well think this fault is a very rare one and of no consequence. I can assure them it is of great consequence to beginners and mediocre players.

For a moment, however, let us leave these shots where the ball scuttles along the ground and, instead, say something about another fault. That is when the ball goes high into the air but covers no distance at all. I would not say that this fault is as common as is to say fluffing or topping. But golfers who are not very good do suffer from it. Skying the ball happens with the wooden clubs, very often when playing against the wind as I have already said. What happens is that the clubhead goes under the ball, or at least with too much of the face of the club striking the lower half of the ball.

With all faults such as fluffing, skying and topping, the root cause of the trouble is swaying or the transferring of weight. I have already mentioned this in connection with fluffing, but it applies to the other two faults I have mentioned as well. However, there is a marked difference between these faults and their relationship to swaying. For in skying the ball the arms have been pushed up quickly and all the weight has been shifted over to the right leg. This means that the body has moved as well, and there is no springboard on which the downstring can be started.

The only way to get the clubhead down is to shift back the weight very quickly and then lunge down at the ball. Consequently the hands lose control and the clubhead comes down quickly, hitting the ground behind the ball and the ball at the same time. In fact, the ball is hit with the top of the club, not the face, and as a result the ball goes more or less straight up in the air.

As I have said, fluffing, topping and skying are all interrelated to some degree, for the bad habit which can cause a golfer to sky the ball, or to fluff or top it, is that the movement of the body as the club is being brought down is too far to the left. You will never sky the ball if the clubhead is taken back low. I defy anybody to do this. Professionals do not agree with each other on every point, but they are all agreed on this.

Back to earth again, and there is the bad habit of topping. Like smothering or fluffing, this causes the ball to trundle along the ground. If such a thing happens on the tee, then more than likely the ball will find its rest in some longer grass or heather in front of your nose a few yards away. On the fairways, it nearly always seems to happen that a ball is topped when there is some hazard in front. I don't know why this should be, unless the golfer is just that little bit anxious, but it does often happen and the result can be quite disastrous.

Lifting the arms on the backswing is one of the main causes of topping the ball. This lifting up the arms is caused by the weight being on the left side going back and then being shifted to the right side coming down. The swaying ruins the whole arc of the swing and the whole concept of bringing the club-head into the ball just at the moment that the clubhead is at its very lowest point. Some professionals say that swaying and lifting the arms are two different things, and unrelated to each other. That is sheer rubbish. The two things are connected, make no mistake about that, although topping can take place even if the arms are raised too quickly, or if there is swaying of the body.

There is another reason for topping the ball. Not looking at it. 'Head Up' is one of the most common faults in golf, and naturally you cannot hit a golf ball correctly without looking at it. I have seen professionals do this for fun. But they are always standing correctly and gripping the club correctly so that hitting a golf ball becomes completely automatic to them. But not even the greatest golfer in the world could hit every time without looking at it. No sir. It can't be done.

So you have to look at the ball. And I want to be quite clear what is really meant by 'Head Up'. Many golfers – good golfers at that – turn their head to the left when hitting the ball, and get away with it because their head turns far too late for any harm to be done. But that is a very different thing from jerking the head up when the clubhead is still being brought down, for the jerking of the head at that moment also causes the shoulders to lift up and the whole swing is completely spoilt. Some say that it is the lifting of the shoulders which causes the head to jerk up, but that is quibbling, for the two things go together in my view, and more than that, they happen together.

I believe the jerking of the head is caused by nervousness, or by anxiety, which is the same thing really. Everybody wants to get the ball well away from the tee if there is a great deal of rough in front, and everybody wants to get the ball well clear of the bunker in front of them. That is why topping frequently occurs in such situations.

Providing that you swing the club reasonably well with your hands, then the reasons for topping are swaying and jerking the head. These are the two things which have to be watched. Remember that you cannot send the ball forward if the weight is on the right foot when the clubhead meets the ball. You must be going after the ball. Correcting faults is a bit of a daft statement when you come to think of it, because the only way to correct faults permanently is to play the right way. And experimenting in golf is very dangerous, for the very simple reason that many golfers do not know what has gone wrong. They may think they do, but that is a very different thing. Now, if you carry out experiments at anything and have no idea of what you are about, how can you possibly get to the correct result? Answer me that. You must know what you are trying to achieve. Just suppose, for instance, that your car was not going very well, and you started mucking about with it to try to make it go better and had no knowledge of car engines. You might be in trouble and so might be your car. And suppose you tried messing around with the electric wiring in your house. You might set the whole place on fire.

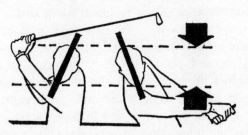

Tilt your head – Don't lift it

The trouble is that most experimenters think they have some knowledge of their subject, and that is worse than having no knowledge. And, believe me, the people who mostly experiment with their golf are those who think they know something about it. Those who know nothing are usually more sensible, and decide to see their pro.

By making the various checks I have been talking about you will get to the root of the trouble. But you will not get to the root of the trouble by fiddling about with your grip and so on. So-called 'cures for faults' are not anything more than temporary measures, and with them it is more than likely that you will go too far, and will get yourself into worse trouble. Certainly, if you develop some bad faults during a round of golf, you just have to get round the course as best you can. The best way to try is to play the game properly, not do all sorts of things trying to right a wrong with another wrong.

Some golfers think that the practice ground is the place for experiments, and so it is if you know what you are doing. It is not a place for meddling with your game if you do not know what you are doing; it is a place for getting your game right by getting back to the proper method of hitting the ball. You have often heard the expression of 'reaching for your goal'. And the goal to reach for in golf is to hit the ball correctly, and in as simple a way as possible.

I can just see some of you say 'That is a lot of nonsense. What about Old Joe Bloggs. He does everything wrong according to the experts, yet he hits the ball and scores well.' All I can say to this is, 'jolly good luck to Old Joe'. Of course, there are golfers around who look like acrobats as they swing a club, and yet hit the ball, just as there are some horses who look like cart horses rather than race horses and yet get over the sticks. But there are millions of golfers playing the game all over the world, and included among them are quite a few unorthodox performers. But you cannot legislate for them. They are a law unto themselves. And anyway, who is to say that, if they played in a simple orthodox fashion, they would not have been far better golfers?

I feel that most if not all that goes wrong in golf is caused by bad thinking or lack of concentration, call it what you will. That is the basic cause of everything, because bad thinking invariably leads to being generally mixed up. That in turn, leads you to rush shots, and that starts it all. We can talk about lifting the head or the shoulders, throwing out the arms and goodness knows what else, but all these things are caused by anxiety and consequently to hurrying. I am not saying that faults cannot creep into golf if the player is unhurried, but the chances of that are not nearly so great.

Then again, the chances of making mistakes are obviously going to affect players with a bad method to a far greater degree than it will affect players with a good method, and I maintain that those with an upright swing will make more mistakes than a player who has a wide arc to his swing.

Just recently there has been a good deal of talk about the American Bert Yancey and his 'square to square' method of hitting a golf ball. I have watched Yancey closely and have also seen him on television, and his way of playing is the same as mine. He takes the club back in a wide arc and there is comparatively little cocking of the wrists. He lets that take care of itself – which is what I am preaching.

There is no doubt that taking the club back low and wide also gives you better balance, and that bad balance – with its consequent wrong weight transference – causes a lot of bad shots to be played. Upright swingers are particularly liable to hurry their shots.

I daresay, too, that to read about so many faults at one go may have depressed some readers. I certainly have no wish to do that, but facts have to be faced, and it would be silly for me to say that once you have learned how to grip and swing the club correctly that is the end of all your problems. Golf, like life, is full of problems, although in the case of golf they are of one's own making.

Stop making problems for yourself, and you will find that golf will be a simpler and an easier game. For instance, I am sure that many golfers think there are many obscure reasons why they fluff and top or sky or smother a ball. The reasons are not obscure at all, as I have tried to point out.

But let us move along, but still in the same department. I want to say something about a fault which, because it creeps into the game when one is near the green is more than usually demoralising. A bad drive or a bad long shot is bad enough, but when a bad shot is played near the green it probably means that from being in a good position the golfer suddenly finds himself in not much better a position after having played one shot more.

The fault I refer to is fluffing when playing little shots near the green. In other words, to hit the ground rather than the ball, which causes the ball to go only about half the required distance. Here playing off the right foot and with loose wrists can cause a fluff, but I feel that a great many bad shots are played because of nervousness. The shot is hurried, with a floppy action. I am not suggesting that you should be all tensed up when you are playing short shots but there must be complete control of the club.

So many golfers think that playing short shots is really a different kind of game to the rest of golf. It is not. It is merely a variation of other shots to suit the circumstances. Nobody, for instance, would dream of taking a great full swing when they were only thirty yards from the green. That would be suicidal. Nor is it necessary to make the ball go high into the air if there is nothing between you and the green. I know some pros do it but they know what they are about. My advice to club golfers is to keep the ball as near to the ground as practicable.

That being so, a No. 5 or a No. 6 iron is sufficient. I know that you will not be able to stop the ball as quickly as you would playing a more lofted club, but all the same you will be able to get the ball on the green and somewhere near the flag.

Take your time for short shots, and be in control of the club. If you still cannot master the shot, then keep your left arm very stiff. I know a lot of pros will laugh at that because it is not the real cure, but at least it will keep you from fluffing shots. Of course, that method is merely one to get you through the rest of the round. After you finish you should go to your professional and get him to sort things out. If you do not do that then you must try the best you can to experiment on the practice ground.

Another tip to see you through the round, or even to employ at other times, is the 'Texas wedge' – which is the American term for using a putter off the green. Some elderly players are very good at this shot. Your pals may laugh at you, of course, but what does that matter if you get results. All the golf teachers in the world can say this and that about correct methods, but golf is a matter of improvisation. How can it be otherwise, when there are tall men, short men, thin men, fat men, strong men, weak men, and players with varying degrees of skill all at the game? Of course there must be improvisation, and the 'Texas wedge' is a case in point.

On looking back at this chapter and going into faults, I think that perhaps the greatest of all golf faults is hurrying the shot. I do not mean to infer that the golf swing should be so slow as to generate no power at all. But hurrying and jerking must lead to disaster. It can't do anything else, can it? If you try to do some odd job in a hurry at home it is more likely that you will make a botch of it, and may have to do it all again. But at golf you don't get any second chances. If you hurry a shot and make a mess of it the shot is lost, perhaps the competition is lost and, more than likely, your temper will be lost. And what does that mean? – more hurrying and more lost shots!

It all builds up, you see, and that is what causes a golfer to go from bad to worse. The best golfers – and the most successful ones – are those who play a bad shot but who do not let it worry them unduly, and who take plenty of time to play their next shot. Ideally, every golfer after making a mistake, should take a little walk by himself – but perhaps that is too much to ask.

So to the putting green. Many, perhaps most, of a golfer's mistakes take place on the putting green, again mostly by hurrying and jerking the putt, because of nervousness or lack of confidence. I have always said that you could hole a putt while standing on your head if you had sufficient confidence to putt that way. But we would all look a bit funny, I admit,

Aim to land on an imaginary green when chipping out of the rough

so I leave the question of putting faults by saying that, as in every other department of the game, a sound method which feels comfortable is the way to successful putting. Having said that, I imagine that golfers will carry on as they have always done – and, as I used to do, experiment with every kind of putting method under the sun, before, more than likely, coming back to the original one. It proves what I have said, that putting is all a matter of confidence.

CHAPTER SEVEN

Dress and Clubs

As I have a reputation of being a smart dresser on the golf course, I should like to say something on that subject. I wear bright clothes because it makes me feel good, and I believe that to be true of any golfer, whether he be a professional or just an ordinary club player. I know that I see youngsters around playing in tournaments who look as if they have been sleeping in their clothes. Poor chaps, some of them might have had to do just that, because they earn nothing as golfers, and for all I know, might have had difficulty in scraping up the price of a bed. But that is another story. Slovenly dressers are slovenly-minded people, and when I see all these long haired layabouts walking about the streets of London when I make one of my infrequent visits there, it frightens me. I know that nowadays long hair is *the* thing and I don't mind long hair if it is tidy. We have long haired chaps in golf now and we have to accept them, but long hair does not make them any better golfers.

I am a tidy man myself, and being tidy in one's person makes one tidy in everything one does. However, golfers are much better dressed than they used to be, and it is not often now that you see all the members of a Sunday-morning four-some going out with their trousers tucked in their socks. That used to make my blood run cold, although years ago I suppose they had little alternative, because then golfing clothing was scarce and had no great variety. Money was probably scarce as well, so golfers had to wear some old pair of trousers that were no good for anything else. But now there is a vast range of golf clothing of all kinds — and smart clothing at that.

My only complaint is that I think there is still room on the market for very light waterproofs that will keep out the heaviest rain, but I suppose there are technical reasons for such articles not being produced just as there will be technical reasons for not producing very light shoes that, after a good deal of service, remain waterproof. I must say, though, that especially in shoes, there has been a great improvement in recent years. When I first started if you wanted shoes to keep out water you had to have a pair which were something like a pair of navvy's boots.

I can remember when my father, Gus, was playing golf, he more often than not wore a thick gaberdine sort of water-proof jacket and trousers — an outfit which he used to tell me was so hot and sticky that he could hardly swing a club when wearing it. On warm days or dry days he wore a drab pullover. That, apparently, was the only choice that he had.

Of course, in those days professionals were down-to-earth characters, and had never heard of a bit of showmanship. Only Hagen and one or two others had thoughts in this direction, before Henry Cotton came along and lifted British professional golf up and gave it a new image by being smartly dressed. British pros owe a great debt to Henry, for that as well as many other reasons. Now they are, in the main, very well and in some instances colourfully dressed. Perhaps I have had something to do with the latter. I don't know, but if I had I am very happy.

Club golfers, those chaps who play golf at week-ends, have been slow to catch on in this dress business. Some of them are very wealthy men, but if the club pro tries to sell them something smart they regard it as an extravagance, and off they go to play in their old waterproof jackets or sweaters. It beats me, it does! Perhaps a wealthy man has no need to dress well to give him confidence, but do you think he would go to his office dressed in any old clothes? Not on your life. After spending a weekend at the golf club in old clothes, on Monday morning he is off to the office in a natty suit with a bowler or a black Homburg hat, and his rolled umbrella, as smart as smart can be. And why? To give him confidence, of course!

I feel that, with many such men, playing golf in old clothes is a case of inverted snobbery. 'You see old So and So, dressed like a scarecrow? He's a millionaire, or pretty well near it, you know'. That is the kind of remark you hear at golf clubs. Well, it takes all kinds to make a world – even eccentric millionaires.

Nevertheless, I maintain that, if you are smartly dressed on a golf course, you feel good – and that applies to everybody, good golfers and bad. It is the psychological approach that is always so important. Do you think your car runs better when it is filthy, or do you think it runs better when it is spanking clean? I always think mine goes better when it is clean. Of course it does nothing of the kind, but I think it does. That is the important thing. It is the same with golf. If you feel good you will feel that you will play better golf – and the chances are you *will* play better. Does it sound crazy? I don't think so.

So much for that then. Now down to reality. Close-fitting warm clothes and loose, flapping clothing can certainly affect you, physically. Supposing, for instance, you go out on the course wearing a tight-fitting waterproof jacket. It is obvious that your movements are going to be restricted. You cannot swing a golf club in that outfit, and any tight clothing can cause you to play bad shots.

It is much the same if your clothing is loose and flapping

111

about. It gets in your way and distracts you. If you see something flapping about out of the corner of your eye just when you are playing a shot something disastrous is bound to follow. And the same happens if you are wearing a loose cardigan, and you feel it slipping off your shoulder. I may be exaggerating a bit, but such untoward things do occur, and believe me, when you are playing golf you do not want your attention drawn elsewhere.

In talking about waterproofs I do not want you to think that modern waterproofs are not efficient and, if you are careful in your choice, not comfortable. But the point is that so many club golfers are wearing waterproof clothing that is out-dated and, more likely than not, ill-fitting. This especially applies to middle-aged golfers, whose figures might have got a little fuller with the passing years. My own weight has not changed much, but then I have always been a fitness fanatic, and for many reasons many golfers do not find the time to be that, although I think that they jolly well should.

By that, I am not suggesting that they should have a five miles run every morning, but that they should take care with their diet, not drink to excess, and that they should, generally, look after themselves. I feel that many, perhaps most, golfers do not change their golf clothing often enough, just as they do not change their golf clubs often enough.

Plus-fours or knickerbockers have gone out of fashion nowadays, and I am one of the few professionals to wear them now that Tom Haliburton plays so little in tournaments. There, incidentally, was a neatly-dressed golfer for you, and a neat golfer as well. I have never seen Tom untidy, ever, and although he never effected the bright colours that I fancy, he was always immaculate. If anybody wanted an example of a tidy golfer whose dress was reflected in his game it was Tom – who has, all his life, been a credit to the game in every way. One could also say the same about Bobby Locke, another credit to the game of golf. He was never untidy in dress, and his game was never untidy either.

Knickerbockers or plus-fours are my type of fashion

I wear knickerbockers because they are neat, because they give freedom of action, and because in wet weather they do not flap around my ankles. Sometimes, if your waterproof trousers have worked up, a little water does run around your ankles, causing a little discomfort. And, if the bottoms of your slacks get wet it causes them to fray, and so they need repairing or renewing.

Going back to shoes. I always think that golf shoes should be cleaned and kept properly. That is easy to do nowadays because of the new synthetic material of which they are made. In the old days, heavy leather shoes had to be scraped, then washed, then oiled, and later polished. But all these new shoes need is a good wash. In ordinary, everyday life, I like to see men with a clean shirt and a clean pair of shoes, and if ever I had been going after a job I would have seen to it that I had a clean shirt and tidy well-polished shoes – for the simple reason these things would have given me the same kind of confidence as the business man who was interviewing me, wearing his smart suit.

So we have two good reasons for being well dressed on the golf course, the first that it helps you psychologically, and the second that your clothing will neither distract you or hamper your movements. To me they seem two good reasons. And don't forget, too, that the spikes in your shoes should be in good order, with none of them missing. Spikes are put into the soles of shoes to give you a good grip and, if there are some missing, the effective grip is all that much less. And do not put your shoes away with a lot of mud or pieces of turf adhering to the spikes. Clean the soles as well as the uppers of the shoes.

What about you golf clubs? Sam King never cleaned his golf clubs or had them cleaned. But Sam was a law unto himself. Like the clean car that I think goes well, I also think that golf clubs should be wiped after each game. Of course, modern clubs do not rust like the old ones, but all the same it is nice to see them gleaming, and some golfers, I must say, after they finish a round of golf treat their golf clubs as if they hated them. After a bad round perhaps they do, but that is hardly fair when the blame should rest on themselves. How many club players wipe their clubs carefully after a round on a wet course, or clean the dirt out of the scores on the faces of the clubs? And not many wipe and dry the grips of their clubs either. Golf clubs in a sense are like motor cars and women, they respond to kindness, and do not respond as well if they are not well treated.

Once you have got good equipment, look after it, and it will serve you well. But do see that you get the right equipment in the first place. It is not good enough, for instance, to go into a pro's shop and buy a set of clubs with a famous name on them. They might suit you but then again, they might not, and in this matter you should try to persuade your professional to have some practice swings with one or two of them. Of course, the professional will tell you which set he thinks might suit you, but, after all, he is not swinging the clubs.

You are the person who is doing that. Very few golfers use clubs which are too light for them – club golfers I mean – but many do use clubs that are too heavy for them. This is something I am very keen on, this too-heavy-club business. Of course, when you are buying clubs the question of cost comes into it as well. If you do not have much money, and if you are a beginner, then you have to do what you think best. The best, in such circumstances, is to build up a set of clubs, good clubs, buying a few to begin with, and then adding to the set as funds and experience permit. Buying an old, second-hand set is not the ideal way of acquiring good clubs, as a rule, but there are times when this has to be done. But for goodness sake, and especially if you buy new clubs, look after them. There may come a time when you want to sell them to get another set, and if your clubs are spick and span you will get a better price for them.

The same argument hardly applies to golf clothing. It is

not sold after you have finished with it or given in part exchange after you are tired of it. But then that applies to everyday clothing as well. However, that is no reason for keeping golf clothing so long that it becomes shabby, and thus reduces your morale on the golf course.

Even if you are one of those characters who don't care about his dress on the golf course, or just flings clubs into the locker after a game without giving them another thought, please try out what I have been saying. I do not say that, if you turn over a new leaf, your handicap will come down by leaps and bounds, but in the long term you might be surprised at the general improvement in your game. At the very least, I think you will get more enjoyment out of golf – and, after all, that is very important whether you play, off scratch, or toddle around trying to play to eighteen. Because you play badly is no reason to dress badly. I am sorry if I am labouring the point, but it seems to me that it is not completely unimportant.

CHAPTER EIGHT

The Mental Side of the Game

The mental side of golf. That covers an awful lot, doesn't it? In fact if I went into it fully, it would take a book all to itself. It's a deep subject, and I doubt if any club golfer, or indeed any golfer, would have it gone into too deeply. All the same, some golfers really don't give themselves a chance to play golf well. They think that they can rush up to the golf club in their car, change as quickly as they can so as not to keep Old Charlie waiting, and before they know where they are they are on the tee and have topped the ball a hundred yards or less in front of them. Oh, I've seen it happen so many times. But that's not the end of the story. They take four or five holes before they recover. By that time they are a few holes down, then they start to press, and all is lost. They're dead. They're beaten, and they come into the bar and moan about it for hours, blaming this thing and the next. Of course they never think of blaming themselves.

Let me say this. In Britain, I am sad to say, too many clubs are still without a practice ground and, say what you like, a practice ground is always some incentive to golfers to go out and hit a few shots, although, Heaven knows, even at clubs with practice grounds all too few golfers use them. But we have to be fair to such golfers. After all, they work in an office all week and when the week-end comes all they can think of is having a couple of rounds on a Saturday and getting two in on a Sunday if the Old Woman will allow it. And as long as they manage to do that they are happy, no matter how they play. All right, they moan about how they play but the great thing is: 'I've got two rounds in today'. That, for the most part, is all they seem to care about.

That is all wrong. They ought to sacrifice a month or so at the start of the season by going on the practice ground doing what I am trying to teach. If they did that they would halve their handicap in a few weeks. But they play week-end in week-end out, playing a couple of rounds a day if they can manage it, and generally speaking they will never get any better. But it is unfortunate that every club has not got a practice ground. This matters little to an awful lot of golfers, but it does matter to those who want to practice. The right answer would be to change their golf club, but that is not always easy either.

When you practice, you have to know what exactly you are trying to do. How often do you see players at a golf club practising to get out of a bunker? There again, very few golf clubs in Britain have a practice bunker. But if I were a member of a golf club and wanted to practice bunker shots I would take myself away to some quiet bit of the course and practice in a bunker. If I were found out that would be just too bad. I would apologise if it were frowned on and be most careful that I was not seen the next time. But, even practising bunker shots, you have to be sure that you know what you are trying to do. So many have no idea how to get out of a bunker. They stand near the ball and try to fluff it out. That is no good at all, as I have explained earlier.

And this brings me to another point. Many club golfers are wasting their time practising for the very simple reason that they are wrong from the word 'go'. They try to correct faults with other faults. I see no redemption for such golfers, because they have become accustomed to swinging their club above their head and snatching at the ball. If they stick to that they can only make the best of a bad job.

I have heard one member of a golf club saying to another, 'You know, George, you were swinging very flat this morning.'

'Was I really?' replies George. 'I had no idea I was.' And he looks utterly miserable.

What a pity, because that was the way that man should have been swinging. I am unable to understand it, but it seems that there is something built in golf that wants to make everybody try to wave a golf club way above their heads. It seems to be the same all over the world – this idea that, if you are not swinging a golf club above your head, you are not swinging it properly. It makes me laugh. It tickles me to death.

To my idea, when you have the clubhead at the top it should be two or three feet from the neck, and you can't do that with an upright swing. The shaft has to be right away from your neck, and if you can get the shaft of the club horizontal round your back, then you are in a perfect position, but the shaft must be laid off the right shoulder, a couple of feet or so away. If they practice that swing then they will do themselves an awful lot of good, but if they listen to the other members talking a lot of rubbish to them and telling them they were swinging too low then there is no hope for them. To go out and try to do what the other members think they should do is a sheer waste of time. They would be far better doing a bit of work in their gardens.

This listening to their friends and then trying to do what the friends say is a matter of confidence to a great extent, or rather a lack of confidence. To have confidence is very important in golf, but only if you are doing the right thing. If you are doing just that, then confidence is everything. And, if you are using the right method, which I say is my method, then you will be surprised at the ease with which you hit the ball. You will be more than surprised. You will get the shock of your life at how the ball flies off without being hit hard at all.

But confidence is a scarce commodity among club golfers. When you listen to their talk, you will realise that they are most depressing people before they start a round. You hear them say: 'I hope I don't play like I played last week', 'I hope I do better than last time', 'I'm not sure – I don't know really what I'm doing wrong'. You very seldom hear them say. 'I feel great, I'm going to play a good round today'. They're always worried. Of course, they play the odd good hole, but that's more good luck than anything else.

It's not lack of concentration that makes so many golfers play badly. A lot of clever people play golf. They can concentrate all right because they are accustomed to dealing with business problems. The trouble is that they're barking up the wrong tree. They are clever men, much more clever than I am, but they haven't a clue as to how to hit a golf ball, and I have. It's sad, very sad, but, after they read this book and do what I tell them to do, their golf troubles, or most of them, should be over. You see, there has never been a golf book like this before. People who have written books either have not known what they are talking about (there have been exceptions, of course) or they have been too frightened to tell the truth about golf for fear they would be laughed at.

Has anybody ever written in a book that most club golfers are wasting their time practising? If there has been such a book I have not read it. But what I say is true. Half the club golfers, or perhaps a good deal more, have no idea what they are trying to do. The ones who do know what they are about are usually older players who swing the club low round their right hip. They fizz the ball away with a half swing back and a half follow-through. It may look terrible to some people, but they do everything correctly, and the ball goes away with a draw and runs like anything. A perfect way of hitting a golf ball.

I am not saying that the swing I am advocating was always used. Certainly, even in the very old days, they had the club horizontal at the top of the backswing but, before the golf ball we have now and before steel shafts, they had to have the right elbow out to get some height on the club so that they could cut away the ball on the downswing. 'The chicken's wing', they called the right elbow, because it stuck out. A good description, I think. It was the only way that they could get the ball away, cutting it away, because you must remember that the ball was a pretty dud affair, and even good hickory shafts were hardly as good as steel shafts. Cutting the ball away was the only way they could ever get it up in the air. If they had not played like that it would have rolled and bounced along the ground.

The introduction of the rubber-cored ball around the turn of the century made a world of difference to the game, but for the most part golfers still use the right elbow out, the 'chicken's wing' method right up to about 1930, when steel shafts became the thing. Then the game changed. But most club golfers don't seem to realise this. They are still taking the club back upright with their right elbow out, and cutting across the ball with a stiffer shaft. It was different in the old days when they flicked the ball away. There was a lot of torsion in a hickory shaft, far more than there is in these stiff shafts nowadays. In the old days you could come down with an open face and the torque of the shaft would throw the clubhead over. It was an easy way of playing golf really, but for the most part you could not get the length, nor, in fact, would you get length now if you were playing one of these old balls using steel-shafted clubs.

The strange thing is that, although old photographs of the great golfers show all sorts of different things, they seem to be doing all of them taking the club back low. This is particularly noticeable in photographs of Harry Vardon in his later years. Then he swung low and round with his right elbow well tucked in, but earlier pictures of him show him

The chicken-wing – or – The flying right elbow

with a much freer right elbow. It could be that he started to change his method gradually after the rubber-cored ball became popular.

Certainly the old chaps seem to have improvised a good deal. They took the club back low, they cocked their wrists and bent their elbow, keeping it well away from them, and had the shaft of the club horizontal at the top of their swing. Then they threw out the club to get it high and to be able to cut across the ball, yet they still managed to get behind the ball. (Remember that the cut given to the ball was mainly caused by the torsion of the shaft.) It all sounds complicated, but to them it appears to have been reasonably simple. Now, with steel shafts and the high-grade balls we play with, you do not have to try to cut the ball away as they had to do years ago.

The trouble is that many, many club golfers think they still have to do some of the things they did years ago, forgetting they do not have to cut the ball away because it will rise after being correctly hit from behind. Heaven knows how this has persisted, but it has, and I believe that it has made for complications in the game, and complications mean that confidence can be affected. Golfers must know what they are trying to do, and must also have confidence in themselves.

We all know that in golf things can go wrong for a variety of reasons, and when things do go wrong what happens to the average club member? He becomes depressed; he loses any fire that was in his belly and, more often than not, just gives up the ghost. This is all wrong, although I know it is easy to say 'Forget a bad hole'. That is not as simple as it sounds. We hear a lot about good golfers being able to forget a bad hole and carry on as if nothing bad had happened. True, tournament players can carry on as if nothing had happened to them like a bad hole, but it is poppycock to say that they forget it. I can only speak for myself, but if I play a really bad hole I just don't forget it. What I do is to push it to the back of the mind, although it has a nasty habit of coming forward again. The one thing you must not do is to let any thoughts of previous disaster intrude on what you are thinking about at the moment, such as playing a shot or trying to hole a difficult putt. If you can put previous troubles out of your mind you are very lucky. The best most people can do is to forget them as soon as possible, and to think of them only when there is nothing on the mind at that moment.

This, I am afraid, is beyond many, many golfers, and so after one bad hole they go on to another, and then another, and their round is a shambles. Golf fanatics have tried this and that to try to cure the despondency which follows a bad hole, but that is not the answer. The answer is *prevention* – to avoid playing a bad hole as far as is humanly possible. There will always be good luck and bad luck in golf, and there are times when a ball can kick badly and you find yourself in a horrible lie after you have played a good shot. There is nothing you can do about it. You have had a rub of the green, and the best you can do is to be economical in the use of shots.

Now here is a situation which requires confidence. Not misplaced confidence which makes you 'Have a Go', but real confidence which makes you plan in your head how you are to get out of trouble, and how you are to get down without an astronomical figure going down on the card. That means thinking not only of the next shot, but of the one after that. It also means you have to decide where the ball is going to land each time. This is the time when so many golfers fall down.

Make no mistake about it, there are times when you have bad luck, although for Heaven's sake don't become one of those golfers – and there are plenty of them – who are always moaning about it. It comes to everybody at times, but those using my method will hit fewer bad shots than the upright swingers. The only time they will hit bad shots is when they have the ball too near the left foot. That is bad,

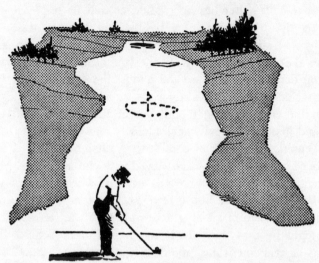

Always aim for a specific spot when driving down an open fairway

for then the ball will be hit on the upswing. I find that to be one of the worst faults, and it has to be watched. If it is not watched, then the ball will be topped or will shoot in any old direction.

When I point out this fault to golfers, they see at once what they are doing and everything is all right. But then, when they go away and they are not careful, the ball gets too near the left foot again, and they say to themselves: 'Blast Faulkner, he's been teaching me all wrong.' So they play another and top it, and say: 'To Hell with Faulkner.' And they play another shot and they top that. Then they say: 'That's it, I'm going back to my old swing.' Then they are back to all their old problems and troubles.

Rather than have the ball too near the left foot I would rather have it too near the right foot, because with the club being in a nose-in position they will never slice the ball. It's impossible to slice, and I will prove it to anyone at any time.

But to go back to this confidence business. It is because the average club golfer has no confidence that he grips the club so tightly. Most grip it so tightly that their knuckles are white with strain. They think that by doing that they are gripping the club confidently. Don't you believe it. All that is being done is to tense up the hands, the arms and, in fact, the whole body. That is not right at all. Golfers should feel that the club is going to fall out of their hands, and they should just have a few waggles loosely and then let go.

Tenseness and lack of confidence go hand in hand. I have noticed it often when I have played with club members. Mind you, almost any club player is nervous when he is playing with a professional, but I have noticed that the least little thing puts them off. It might be having to wait on a shot, or it might be that they are being pressed from behind. This kind of reaction is just mind over matter, and shows complete lack of confidence. I see at once that they are finished – they become so agitated. If they feel they are being pressed they will say, 'Oh, I don't think I'll finish the hole', or even, 'I don't think I'll play this hole'.

You can't play golf that way. You have to be relaxed, with a loose grip and an unhurried swing just sweeping the ball away. But no! The grip gets tighter, the muscles stiffen up, the body gets tense and the game is in bits. If golfers tend to do that, what they should do is to say, 'Let these people through', and after that take their time. The great professional, George Duncan, once wrote a book which I think was called *Golf at the Gallop,* and I have often heard my father say that George Duncan was the fastest golfer he had ever played with. All I can say is that George Duncan must have been a very remarkable man to have played golf so quickly and also to have played it so well. But that is not for everybody. In fact, I would say it is only for the very few who know what they are trying to do and, furthermore, know they can do it. It is the difference between playing golf quickly because of supreme confidence, and playing golf quickly because one is all tensed up. In general, quick golf is not to be recommended, although, Heaven knows, some players nowadays are much too slow. Slowness, in turn is not a good thing either, because it can also lead to tenseness, certainly among club golfers, for it is not their natural game.

Take a man like Bobby Locke who was surely one of the most relaxed men who ever played golf. He was never tense, not even before starting a round. He used to get out of bed in plenty of time, shave leisurely, take plenty of time for breakfast and then drive to the club at about thirty-five miles an hour, never faster. When he arrived at the club, he was calm and unruffled. That is the way to do it. So, if you are playing golf, do the same as Locke used to do, and don't go on the tee all worked up so that you will hurry your shots. If you are tense, then you will swing quickly and you will have the club upright before you know where you are.

There are other golfers who go to play a round still thinking about some business problem or another, or think about where they are going at night, or a dozen and one other things. Too much brainwork must add up to tension in some kind of way. The ideal is for the mind to be completely blank when you set out for a round of golf, completely blank so that the only thing that has to be thought about is pulling the clubhead back along the ground and swinging round the hip. All that fussing and fiddling about is absolutely wrong. I remember when I was a boy we used to play a game, have a competition if you like, when we had to say how many things you could do at one time. That is all right for a kid's game, but it is no good for golf. Yet thousands of golfers would seem to think the more things they have to think about the better their game will be. Did you ever hear such nonsense? But they do, and no wonder there are so many bad players about.

I have had pupils and have told them only one thing, how to take the club back correctly. They have gone away and, before long, are playing much better. Yet it has come back to me that they have said to fellow members, 'I just cannot understand it. Faulkner told me about one thing and one thing only.' I know they feel they have been cheated because I told them just one thing. They think I should have filled their head with all kinds of rubbish and should have taken an hour to do so. Then they think they would have had value for money. And this, I am sorry to say, seems to be the attitude of golfers everywhere.

They have their lesson, or lessons, and have been told this theory and that theory. They are still unable to hit the ball off the ground, but that does not seem to matter. If I were to do that, they would go into the bar and say, 'I've just had a wonderful lesson from Faulkner. He's told me this and he's told me that.' And he buys another round of drinks and goes on and on. The fact that he has not improved his game one little bit makes no difference. I tell them what they should do, and it doesn't take me long to say it. But, human nature being what it is, they think I have failed to spot what they are doing wrong. They think they haven't had a lesson. My reply to that is what I have made the theme of this book – what I teach is a simple, foolproof way of playing golf so that a player's handicap is reduced. As I see it, that is what a golf professional's work is all about.

Not long ago I was speaking to a Scottish international whose game went wrong and who went to another pro. He was given so much theory to think about that since then he's been all to pot, finished. And he's not the only player of great promise who has had his confidence sapped by stupid theories. But I said enough about that earlier on. The reason I am mentioning it again is that it makes my blood boil. You cannot have confidence if you are all mixed up.

Nowadays you hear and read about 'mixed-up kids'. By the look of them, a good many are all mixed up, but they are hardly any more mixed up about life than golfers are about their game. If you have difficulty in believing that, then just stand for some time on the first tee at your club some Sunday morning – one of those Sunday mornings when you have got up early and not rushed to the club! – and you will see what I mean. You will see players swinging, fiddling about, playing about with their grips. Then, when they stand up to the ball to hit it, they will be standing erect, bending forwards, crouching, swaying, twisting. In fact you will see the lot. You will also see a great many more poor drives than good ones.

I do not mean to say that all club golfers are bad, for the term 'club golfers' really means everybody who plays in a club, although through the years it has rather come to imply low-handicap players. There are many good golfers in every club, and they are the golfers who have kept their game simple and natural. I have been labouring this point a great deal in these pages, but I make no apology for that, because it cannot be hammered home too much.

I am conscious that what I have written will not please everybody who will see in my writing much which is opposed to what they think and, in the case of professionals, what they teach. All I say is, 'Give my method a try'. It is a method based on commonsense, and after all golf is, or should be, a game of commonsense. There is no mystery about it. The object is to hit the ball as far as you can as straight as you can. I saw on television the Moon man, Shepard, hitting a golf ball which apparently went for miles in the atmosphere up there. But we are not playing golf on the Moon, yet, so we have to find the proper way to hit a golf ball on a golf course on Earth. I think that my way is the proper way, and have much evidence to support my view, despite what many people might think.

After all, I have been in golf a long time, and have not done so badly, although if I had known years ago what I know now I would have done better. Golf is a simple game, and now I know that it is those who play it who have made it less so. If I have been able to put across in these pages that message then I shall be happy. I mean that, honestly and sincerely.

POSTSCRIPT

Golf in Middle Age

Golf in middle age is a subject that I am very familiar with. It is also a subject about which I am asked frequently. Is playing golf when you have reached fifty or thereabouts a different game from that played by younger people? There are two answers to this question. Yes and No. For myself, I play just the same as I always did, except that, with the passage of years and with my study of the game, I now play simpler. But then I am quite a fit man, and I feel as strong as I ever did. That is because I lead an outdoor life and have always kept myself fit.

But it is not always easy to do that if you work in an office, and for a very simple reason. When you get older the body does not burn up food at the same rate as it did, but the chances are that you are eating the same amount of food, perhaps more, if you happen to like the good things in life. The result is that the old waistline gets bigger, and extra weight means a loss of energy. I have been a fanatic about keeping fit, but I realise that working indoors makes it difficult to do that, and so does the pressure of business which comes to many in middle age.

Such golfers, then, have to do something about their golf game, because they are not as supple as they were, and not as strong as they were. The trouble is that they try to keep on in the way they have also kept on, and this is where many go wrong. They try to get more power to make up for the loss of length which has come to them, and start to sway and heave at the ball in a way which is silly really, because this puts them off balance. You know what I mean, for there is hardly a day goes by but you see old men staggering about like a drunk after they have hit the ball. It's a bit pathetic, really, for some of them have been good golfers in their earlier days. Now they are bad, very bad, and there is no need for them to be, no need at all.

Behind their thinking is the memory, when they were younger, they got up on their toes. This they are still trying to do, and it won't work. Middle aged golfers should forget all about that if they are of the breed who have put on weight and are not so fit. What they should do is to keep their left foot firmly on the ground throughout the swing. That is a dangerous thing to do, when a player has a big turn of his hips and shoulders, but it has to be remembered that when a player is older, fatter and stiffer he does not turn the hips and shoulders to anything like the same extent that he once did. His swing is shorter, and, if he hits against a firm left side with the left foot on the ground, he will get round the course at least to his satisfaction. For those who have let themselves go a bit more than is usual and, for that matter, than is wise, they might do well to try to keep their both feet firmly on the ground. It's all against the principles of golf, of course, but all the same the ball will be off down the middle of the fairway, and that is very important to older players. Three moderate shots played in that manner are better than a couple of bad ones into the rough, because older golfers just haven't got the strength to get out of long grass, heather and the like.

Many older golfers who feel that they have not the strength

they once had change over to the two-handed grip, and this is not a bad idea, for the chances are they do not use their fingers as much as they used to. That being so, with their shorter swing, the two-handed grip can be quite successful. If the overlapping grip has been used for many years some may have trouble in adjusting themselves to a new one, but it really does not take long, and it does ensure that the right hand is stronger than it would otherwise be. But if it is felt that the overlapping grip is working quite well, then don't change it, for in middle age golf is even more of an individual game than it is for younger players.

That is why a great amount of improvisation is needed when some of the length has gone. And very good some of the old boys are at it, too. There is hardly a middle-aged golfer who has not said to himself, 'When I could hit the ball a long way I didn't have the experience to play short shots correctly. Now when I have the experience I can't hit the ball as far as I used to.'

That is very true, and it is a jolly good thing that the short shots don't present the same problems as they once did. Judging distance is not the same problem to older golfers as it is to younger ones, nor is the choice of clubs. After years of playing, every golfer knows just what he can do with a particular club, and, more than that, he knows the right time to use it. Gone, also, is the tendency to try experiments, or to play fancy shots up in the air. Most older players have one thing firmly in their minds, and that is to keep the ball as near to the ground as practicable, which is why you see so many of them using the run-up shot to the green, and using it very successfully. Many a middle-aged player can take the pants off a youngster by saving shots round the green, mainly because he plays a safe shot with the right club and, more than that, because he never hurries his shots, either.

On the green, the older chaps are usually pretty good because they use an economical putting style, which they have got to perfection over the years. In fact – on the putting green, as elsewhere on the course – they look entirely comfortable, which is just what they are. A pity that it takes so many golfers so long to realise that being comfortable in playing golf is half the battle.

I believe, however, that many elderly golfers would stave off their decline at the game were they to use the right clubs. This many of them fail to do, because they are, for the most part, playing with clubs they bought years ago, and the fact of the matter is that these clubs are more often than not far too stiff in the shafts. I am sick and tired of telling some of my elderly friends that, but do you think they listen? No, they don't. They still try, and pretend that they are as strong as ever they were, and that the clubs they played with years ago – having served them well then – will still serve them well.

I suppose it is a form of conceit, really, or perhaps I should be kinder and call it pride. But, whichever it is, many middle-aged players will stick to their clubs. There could be another reason, of course, the fact is that they feel they should not spend a lot of money on new clubs. There is some sense in that, but if they want to enjoy their golf to the end of their playing days, they will do so much better with clubs with whippy shafts. It stands to reason, doesn't it?

Naturally they cannot move the clubhead as fast as they used to, or many of them can't. The swing is shorter, so the speed of it is down to a snail's pace. The only way that it can be quickened up is by whippier shafts. The fact is that many younger golfers who are not too strong in the hands also use clubs with shafts that are far too stiff, never mind the elderly or middle-aged ones. I find it very hard to persuade some elderly golfers that this is so, because I think they imagine that they can give the ball a better thump with a stiff-shafted club, and forget that, when some strength has gone, timing becomes even more important.

On the subject of clubs, older golfers must forget the kind

of shots that they used to play. Presumably they have played on the same course for years and know every blade of grass on it, every tree, every bush, so they remember where they used to hit the ball, perhaps level with some bush or tree, or that they used to clear a certain bunker. They have to forget all that, and remodel their thinking as regards distance, if they are the kind of players who have lost something in this direction. They cannot afford to be adventurous any more – they must settle for playing safe every time. A young and strong golfer can overcome a bad shot to some extent by hitting the next one a tremendous blow. But older players cannot do that.

The choice of which club is to be used is, therefore, of vital importance. Fortunately, with the passage of years, they have got past the stage of feeling embarrassed at having to play a bigger club when someone is playing one or two clubs less. If they have not got over that, then it is high time that they did. Keeping up with the Joneses has nothing to do with the game of an elderly golfer. He has to play his own, well thought-out game. And it is not a bad thing, either, to have a favourite club – such as a spoon or a No. 3 iron to use to chug along the fairway. By doing that, some players might sigh for the old days – but this is fatal. If the power has gone, then the old boys must settle for a different kind of game – a game from which they are going to get maximum enjoyment. After all, there are plenty of veterans out on the course every day, although they are into their eighties, and I seem to remember that a few years ago some golfer was given free golf for life on his ninetieth birthday.

Something else I would advise for those who are really getting on a bit is that they should leave some of their clubs in the locker and take out only seven or eight. Such a number is easier for them to carry or pull round, and it has the advantage of being almost on speaking terms with the clubs that they use.

There have been a number of books written telling middle-

aged golfers just how they can play, but really the secret
is for such golfers to play well within their capabilities. At
their age it is not a case of trying to improve their game – it
is merely a matter of arresting the decline and making up for
a loss of power by other means, such as commonsense and
cunning.

All this has been addressed to those who have put on a bit
of weight, grown older, and become a bit less fit than they
once were. But there are plenty of middle-aged golfers who
are still very fit, and my advice to them is to carry on as
they have always done except, perhaps, that they should not
play with very stiff shafts, and that they should not play with
clubs which are too heavy for them. I have a bee in my
bonnet about this, because I feel most or many golfers of
all ages play with clubs which are too heavy for them. Shafts
are certainly lighter than they were a few years ago, and it
may be that the golf-club manufacturers are at last seeing
the light in this direction. I hope so, anyway.

Let me also say there is no reason for elderly golfers to
become despondent, which I feel so many of them do when
they see their handicap going up. What they have to do is
to be sensible about things, and readjust their game if it needs
to be readjusted. Having played golf for years, as most of them
have done, has also brought with it many compensations,
particularly as regards the short game, and any man who
can roll three shots into two around the green is, for the most
part, a hard man to beat – as many younger players know
to their cost. A sharp, short game, allied to a safe game on
the fairway, is not a bad combination, so stop trying to kid
yourself that you can employ the same methods that were
employed ten or twenty years ago.

Such tactics can only accelerate your downfall, ruin your
scoring and give you apoplexy. And, Heaven knows, there
are an awful lot of elderly golfers who try their best do all
three. Yet many of these men are successful business men,
who are as shrewd and clever as you like at their office, but

who seem to go mad on the golf course and lose their heads completely. Mind you, older golfers are not the only ones who do that, but the point is that there is less excuse for them, because they have been through the mill so many times. Anyway, at their age, they should know better.